HM22 .G3 W432 1987 C.1 STACKS 1987

```
HM      Ferrarotti, Franco.
22
G3      Max Weber and the
W432      crisis of western
1987      civilization
```

$24.50

	DATE	

© THE BAKER & TAYLOR CO.

MAX WEBER
and the
CRISIS OF
WESTERN CIVILIZATION

Franco Ferrarotti

COLLEGE FOR HUMAN SERVICES
LIBRARY
345 HUDSON STREET
NEW YORK, N.Y. 10014

ASSOCIATED FACULTY PRESS, INC.
Millwood, N.Y. / New York City / London

ASSOCIATED FACULTY PRESS, INC.

STUDIES IN SOCIAL THOUGHT:
Polity and Civil Society

Series Editors: Arthur J. Vidich, *New School for Social Research and* Stanford M. Lyman, *Florida Atlantic University*

Glassman, *Democracy and Despotism in Primitive Societies*
Ferrarotti, *Max Weber and the Crisis of Western Civilization*
Ferrarotti, *A Theology for Nonbelievers*
Blustone, *Max Weber's Theory of the Family*

Copyright (c) 1987 by Associated Faculty Press, Inc. All rights reserved. No part of this publication may be reproduced, stored in a retrieval system, or transmitted, in any form or by any means, electronic, mechanical, photocopying, recording, or otherwise, without the prior written permission of the publisher.

Manufactured in the United States of America

Published by
Associated Faculty Press, Inc.
Millwood, New York

Library of Congress Cataloging in Publication Data

Ferrarotti, Franco.
   Max Weber and the crisis of western civilization.

   (Studies in social thought: polity and civil society series) (National university publications)
   Bibliography: p.
   Includes index.
   1. Weber, Max, 1864-1920. 2. Sociology.
3. Sociology—Methodology. 4. Civilization, Occidental.
I. Title. II. Series.
HM22.G3W432   1987   301'.092'4   84-16802
ISBN 0-8046-9382-X

CONTENTS

1. THE METHOD, OR CONCEPTS PLUS TECHNIQUES..........1

2. ETHICAL NORMS AND ECONOMIC BEHAVIOR...........30

3. THE PROBLEM OF POWER...........................56

4. THE SOCIOLOGY OF UNIVERSAL RELIGIONS...........74

5. THE MODERN WORLD AND ITS DESTINY:
   From "Disenchantment" to "Steel Cage"..................98

   NOTES..125

   BIBLIOGRAPHY.................................132

   INDEX..135

ABOUT THE AUTHOR

Franco Ferrarotti, who since 1961 has held the first chair established for Sociology at an Italian university, is Professor of Sociology at the University of Rome. He has also served as Visiting Professor at a number of American universities, notable among them the New School for Social Research and New York University. He is the author of numerous books, several of which have previously been translated into English, including *Toward the Social Production of the Sacred* (1977), *An Alternative Sociology* (1978), and *Max Weber and the Destiny of Reason* (1980). Another of his books, *A Theology for Nonbelievers: Post-Christian and Post-Marxist Reflections,* will also appear in this Associated Faculty Press series in 1987.

PREFACE

Max Weber has been the victim of memorable misunderstandings. A passionate human being has been transformed into a detached, cold-blooded observer. In this book I "use" Max Weber to clarify a twofold crisis: the crisis of social science and the crisis of advanced industrial societies. Social science is plagued by its success. Apparently to speed up its progress, it has divorced method from substance. But in this way, while lightmindedly tackling all sorts of issues, it has lost its sense of relevance and its historical awareness. Industrial societies, on the other hand, have been developing, as Weber had correctly anticipated, on the basis of a reductive view of rationality that seems unable to provide a sense of direction and a common meeting point for diverging interests. Under these conditions societies break up and the Hobbesian *homo homini lupus* gains ground. In this perspective Weber's lesson has an enduring value.

This book is a loose sequel to my earlier study, *Max Weber and the Destiny of Reason* (M. E. Sharpe, 1982). All the quotations, although checked against the original German text, refer to the Italian translations. I wish to thank Arthur J. Vidich, the co-editor of the series, and Richard Koffler and Elizabeth Bigelow of Associated Faculty Press, for their encouragement, helpful advice, and patient, understanding cooperation.

Rome, July 24, 1986

CHAPTER ONE

THE METHOD, OR CONCEPTS PLUS TECHNIQUES

1. Why Max Weber Is a Classic.

Sixty-four years after his death, Max Weber remains a towering figure in the field of the social sciences. From economic sociology to the sociology of religions, from studies on the processes of modernization to systems theory and the methodological debate, there is no area of research in which the works of Weber are not widely quoted and discussed. Why is this so? I think it has happened for two basic reasons: first, because Weber stands at the intersection of the two currents that have most deeply influenced the rise and development of the social sciences, and especially of sociology: positivism and historicism. Second, Weber sought an answer to fundamental questions and was concerned with problems that involved every contemporary society. Where is Western civilization going? What of the concept of capitalism and its relationship to the Protestant ethic? What is the rationale of life and of bureaucratization?

The influence of Weber, which is incontestable and important, is, however, no guarantee that those who extol him have an understanding of his deep purpose and method of working. Indeed, it might well be said that Weber has been more used than understood. Philosophers and historians, economists and sociologists, have latched on to him. In this connection, it is interesting to note that there has never been a Weberian school nor can Weber be described as the leader of a movement. He remained a solitary intellectual scholar, for whom scientific research never took on any of the typical aspects of either teamwork or an industrial enterprise.

2 / WEBER AND THE CRISIS

Who, then, was Max Weber? He was certainly a sociologist, but only in the classic sense of this ambiguous term. He was not a sociologist in the contemporary, restrictive sense—that is, he was not a specialist. His name belongs in the front ranks—in fact, they are not many in number— of encyclopedian sociologists. Weber knew thoroughly and moved freely from economics to law to history to philosophy to methodology. Endowed with an infinite erudition, he mastered in respect to every subject an impressive amount of data from which he drew categorizations and logico-explanatory constructs, "ideal types," terms of reference, "laws," and predictions. But what must at once be clarified is the fact that Max Weber was never a pure methodologist. Methodology for him was never presupposed. It was never produced a priori, never "deduced." In his studies there is nowhere the necessarily constricting, limiting weight of preconstituted categories. The instruments of research grow; they develop; they are sharpened; and finally, they become definitive alongside the growth and development of the research.

What makes Weber great is the sense of problem, the problematic awareness that expresses itself in a series of pressing questions which return as basic leitmotifs in all his writings and seek empirical verification, a basic of intersubjective validity. Why do men obey? What are the effects of ethics, seen as a "lived ethic," on economic behavior? In what sense can one reconcile standardized impersonal procedures of administrative routine with political decision-making and technological innovation? What is to be the future of capitalism and its peculiar "spirit"? What will happen to the realm of ideas, to the great values of the liberal tradition, that for Weber made up the heart of Western civilization?

This broad, evocative problematic does not remain in Weber at the level of an abstract, philosophizing formulation. If this were true, we would have in him a brilliant essayist or a philosopher of history of the traditional kind, and not a sociologist. What makes him a sociologist is the attempt to join together the general propositions, in which his problematic awareness is evident, with empirical indicators—or with parameters tied to the systematic gathering of empirical data which, in the outline of the project, help to verify or falsify the working hypotheses, be they general or specific. Here it is that one crosses the line that differentiates the sociologist from the essayist or the philosopher. In sociology, the philosophical, highly personal impulse, as a reflex of existential experience and of values or principles of the preference of each individual researcher, must tend to be transmuted into a tried, scientific proposition—one that is *no longer personal, but intersubjectively valid* as a public procedure rather than a private conviction.

The criticism that Talcott Parsons leveled at Weber is thus wholly unjustified. Parsons complained that Weber, in outlining the types of social action on the basis of the determining criterion of action itself, stops with four types (traditional, rational in regard to ends, rational in regard to the active subject, affective or emotive), and did not, on the other hand, try—as he himself wanted to do, believing that he was fulfilling the interrupted work of Weber—to deduce by general defining premises all possible types of social action. Parsons's reproof, in fact, points up one of Weber's great merits. Weber did not deduce all possible types of social action for the simple reason that *he did not invent problems,* but cultivated them as analyzed and lived in the historical horizon in which he found himself living. He refused to construct an abstract model of social action without precise empirical reference, which would necessarily have constituted an evasion—if not, in fact, the abolition—of history, and at the same time would have frozen the existing situation taken in its global dimension as an insuperable *nec plus ultra.*

Parsons's lack of understanding of Weber is not a random happening. It is a symptomatic and instructive fact. Let us try to determine its meaning. All Parsons's intellectual endeavor is intended to outline the basic characteristics of the "social system," or to elaborate the evolving universals that ought to be necessary for any society if it is to be capable of functioning at an acceptable level of efficiency. When however, one begins to look closely at these evolutionary universals, one sees that they seem "cut to order," so as to demonstrate the institutional structure and the ideological orientations of the United States of America. These evolutionary universals of Parsons are, in fact, four in number: (1) bureaucratic organization, (2) money and the system of the market, (3) universalist, generalized juridical systems, and (4) democratic associations. Far from synthesizing the ideal of any human coexistence, along with the "functional prerequisites" of any technically advanced society, the characteristics described by Parsons are seen to be *prima facie* what they are: an extrapolation in general terms—and ingenuous as is obvious by its very language—of some aspects of the American way of life, passed off as the aspects par excellence of the mode of life of any technically advanced society, whereas we are dealing only with the typical aspects of a determinate historical phase. In this sense, if it is true that by this means Parsons achieves the position of the first prime apologist for the "system of free enterprise," it is also true that his attempt involves trying to block history by eternalizing a specific phase.

Nothing could be further from the letter and the spirit of Max Weber. Weber's sensibility toward history, toward its incessant flux and the multiple infinite richness of life, was extreme. Open and insistent as Parsons's attempt is to close off the historic flow and the unpredictability of its results in the short term of an unverifiable modeling, to the point of impoverishing them in schemes of a sociological reasoning which is basically teleological, so, on the other hand, Weber's analysis is both subtle and penetrating in dealing with relations between sociology, positivism, and historiography.

We have already remarked above that the importance of Weber is precisely to be seen in the position that he occupies at the intersection of these worlds of thought, basic for setting up and developing the modern social sciences. Now, let us see clearly what this means at both the level of theoretical conceptual elaboration and of field research.

2. How to Use the Classics

For this operation, it is necessary to take one's distance. Max Weber is a classic; the classics are useful but also dangerous. All classic writers must be treated with respect: the reading of their writings must be carried out in the framework of the context in which they lived, thought, and worked. In this sense, and under these conditions, this becomes a reading which is more than philologically correct; it is also critical. The art of using the classics also demands, however, a certain degree of freedom and familiarity before them, the ability to ask embarrassing questions of them, to evaluate what in them is alive and enduring and what ephemeral — a "freedom from reverence," or in other words, the freedom to reconstruct their thought and their mode of intellectual life in constant relation to modern problems.

Therefore, neither superficial demystification nor hagiography, but careful objective study, open toward both past and present, is required.

If this holds true, by and large, for all classics, and if the ability to withstand such study and to emerge undiminished lies at the root of their lasting validity, then this is preeminently true of Weber, who was extraordinarily aware of the inevitable fate of obsolescence which all scientifically serious work must face. While the creative work of the writer, the poet, in some way challenges the centuries and deals with ever-present universal problems and tensions of humanity as such, on a relatively metahistorical level—becoming part of what has rightly been called the "common heritage of mankind—matters are quite different from the scientist. In regard to creative, artistic discussion which in itself has motives for its own validity, scientific discourse is valuable only insofar as it presents a logical progression in relation to all known preceding explanations, and at the same time, prepares the indispensable preconditions for its own transcendence. Indeed, scientific discourse finds its basic meaning in the characteristic of internal self-correctability.

There is in this aspect of modern scientific activity a highly valuable sense of the extent and the limit, as well as a realization of the necessary precariousness or provisional nature of its own contributions, which, not surprisingly, elicited from Weber a response of harsh stoicism. "A really 'completed' work of art is never transcended; it never ages: the individual can personally give it a meaning of a different value, but of a work which is really completed in the artistic sense, no one can ever say that it has been transcended by another work even if that has been 'completed.' Vice versa, each of us knows that in science his own work, after ten, twenty, or fifty years, has aged. This is the destiny—or better, this is the *meaning*—of scientific work, to which, as regards all the other elements of culture of which one might say the same, is it subjected and entrusted in a totally specific sense: every work of science which is 'completed' involves new 'problems' and must age and be 'transcended.' Anyone who wishes to serve science must be resigned to this."[1]

What are the theories, the ideas, the theoreticoconceptual apparatuses which Weber elaborated and which still today are seen to be useful in research and critical reflection in the sciences? At this point one has to introduce a very important distinction. A social scientist, or a student of social problems, attains the stature of a classic not only and not so much by reason of the permanent validity of his basic theories, necessarily connected with problems of his time and place and thus subject—as we stated above—to a rate of obsolescence which is fairly considerable, but rather by reason of the method of proceeding in the construction of his theories and of the totality of knowledge acquired and experience existentially exploited in the concrete development of his inquiry. (We have delayed to the later parts of this book an analysis of the basic theories of Weber and our judgment regarding their explanatory and predictive capacity.) It is now possible, however, to state that Weber clearly departs from the median of social commentators under the double aspect of his method of construction of theory and of personal preparedness. This has allowed him to gather together the main elements present in the positivistic tradition and in the historicist tradition and thereby to attempt, with largely positive results, an original synthesis of them.

In the first place, there is a striking characteristic in his method of working, which seems extremely far from—if not wholly on principle extraneous to—the modern professional in the field of sociology. The man who seems to be the theorist of "value freedom"—that is, of the absolute distancing between the researcher and the object of research, and between the method and the theme of the inquiry—is instead a man who personally suffers these problems, and who involves himself, especially in the first phase of his scientific activity, in the burning questions of contemporary life, polemicizes with his colleagues, publishes only essays that seem destined to be to be directed to ephemeral situations, and in no way lets his purpose of systematic analysis become visible—a purpose that was later to become visible in the powerful work "*Economy and Society.*"[2]

From the beginning of his career as a scholar, this German professor did not work at all like a professor, still less like a German. Between one nervous breakdown and the next, he worked like a poet: a poet who expends all his energies and the entire lifetime allotted to him, to demonstrate scientifically—that is, by making use of empirical materials that could be checked by everyone—a number of most incisive insights. These were the influence of ethics as lived—that is to say, ethics not as a theoretical system but as an actual influence on daily behavior—on economic life and its forms of development, and vice versa. This was taken as an exemplary case of reciprocal conditioning: the growing power of bureaucratic apparatuses, which, quite independent of ideologies, and indeed with an almost complete indifference toward their regard, seemed destined to accompany the process of modernization and rationalization of social life and the affirmation of mass industrial societies.

3. A Patient Intellectual Craftsman

"Value freedom" *(Wertfreiheit),* which Weber discusses, should therefore be understood in its correct meaning. It is certainly not an invitation to moral indifference or absolute relativism. The tart and in many ways ungenerous criticisms that Leo Strauss brought against Weber in this regard strike at a convenient caricature. But Weber is merely grazed. How can one accuse him of wanting to be "purely objective" and not recognizing the very real reality of "values"? Strauss, as the cautious subtle philologist, the "slow reader" that he is, seems to have enjoyed drawing up what in his view are the conclusive proofs of the contradictory nature of Weber's position: the evaluative adjectives ("rich," "noble," "incomparable," and so forth) in which his work abounds.[3] One can easily move to the demonstration of the necessity of "ultimate values," not quantifiable and not necessarily present in any analysis of a scientific or philosophical type, values of which one cannot "liberate oneself," as Weber on the other hand believes.

Strauss's criticism has, certainly, some weight with regard to the general terms of the world of thought in which Weber moved: that is, to the values of the European liberal tradition that Weber tends to take for granted and to regard as firmly acquired forever, while contemporary history was to demonstrate them the day after his death in all their tragic fragility. He shows himself, however, to be singularly shortsighted about Weber's deep purpose and the general orientation of his personality as a man and scholar. Strauss ends up confusing him with the bustling superficial crowd of modern technicians in the service of the social sciences. Instead, we are dealing with a personality—that of Weber—radically different, endowed with a double characteristic which made up his fundamental matrix. Weber had an extraordinarily intense political temperament, and at the same time the tendency and the real capacity of imposing and giving weight to a total rejection of his own personal feelings when faced with the beauty of nature, of artistic creation, or the truth of science. Mixed together in Weber, there the distinctive traits of the zealous Calvinist and the ardent Judaic prophet. This clarifies his defenseless living out to the utmost the contradictions of his age—his choice of solitude, his lack of political success, his constant struggle against corruption, his political ambiguity, the dissimilation and at the same time frank and dramatic recognition that, alongside and sometimes beyond the supreme ethic of principles, one must find the courage to apply an ethic of responsibility so that the social machinery and the apparatus of the state do not jam. His life illustrates the courage of deciding before having all the reasons at hand, and the scientific demonstration of the rationality of one's own decision—the courage to "dirty one's hands."

What Weber could not accept was subordination to little personal or corporative interests, the triumph of the *camarilla*. It is on this level that his proposed "value freedom" achieves its whole meaning and its polemical significance. A reading of Weber, if it is to be critical and plausible, can only be a historic one. As I have elsewhere noted, one must be aware that the criterion of "value freedom" on which Weber places so much weight, historically helped him as a polemical arm against university colleagues— Treitschke, for example—who used their professional position to spread their personal beliefs.[4] Naturally Weber would have had nothing to which to object regarding those colleagues who would put forth, even from their professorial chairs, their personal points of view and opinions that were personal. What Weber violently reacted against was ideological fraud— that is, the exhibition and propagation of strictly personal points of view as thought these dealt with scientific truths with intersubjective validity. Weber not only denies personal points of view; perfectly logically, in view of his methodological individualism, he believed that one could not do scientific research except by departing from presuppositions which necessarily reflect personal interests and directly involve the researcher. What must be firmly kept in mind, however, is the distinction between point of view and the presupposition from which the research starts and the scientific outcome of the research itself. Furthermore, these very value judgments are a social fact. The misunderstanding into which many critics and interpreters of Weber fall is that one cannot deal objectively with value judgments insofar as they constitute social facts. It is on the basis of the clarification of this misunderstanding that one can—aside from Leo Strauss—understand the peculiar mistake of Theodor W. Adorno, who ends up by putting Weber in the company of a strict positivist like Emile Durkheim. Far from being a Durkheimian *chosiste*, Weber is exactly the opposite of the paleopositivist and noncommitted man of science.

4. The Shame of Commitment

From that point of view, the distance between Weber and the great majority of modern sociologists seems almost insurmountable: it requires a qualitative leap. Precisely because he is the diametric opposite of the noncommitted man of science, Max Weber does not expect that the market will show him themes for research or suggest, even with appropriate commissions, scholarships, financing from foundations, subsidies from enlightened industrialists, what problems it is worthwhile concerning oneself with. As man and scientist, Weber was a person of integrity who bore within himself the reasons for his own autonomy and who found within himself the reasons for the guidance of his own work. He himself asked what were the living problems of his own time and what were the most important questions, those that one could even dedicate a whole life to studying. This is certainly not the case for modern professionals in sociology. It is not by chance that Max Weber has been so crudely misunderstood and dismissed by them. The erroneous conception of "value freedom" in Weber, which reduces it to a programmatic indifference in regard to the subject, is perfectly suited to the needs of those who wait for an indication of themes of research with which to concern themselves on the behalf of clients and the market. This systematic separation between the commitment of the researchers and the object of the research lies at the root of the rise of "sociological fashions," or the fragmentariness and essential gratuitousness of much contemporary sociological research. The problem goes beyond the terms of methodological discussion and becomes a political problem; it implies and involves the self-image and the social function of the sociologist. We cannot confront this, not even in its most general terms, in the present work. We have touched upon it only because it helps to illuminate in a clearer way Weber's method of working and his personality. The "value freedom" of which he speaks is thus not a flight from the responsibilities of the sociologist: it cannot be duly exploited as an excuse for indifference to problems and for a reduction of sociology to a mere technique of social engineering in the service, by definition, of whoever pays best.

The meeting points between the sociologist who will not accept being declassed into a simple technician, and value judgments, are numerous. To start off with, one thinks of the choice of research theme. How does a sociologist begin? How does he or she select one theme from among others? Who—what forces, what social groups—and on the basis of what criteria—determine and justify this choice?

Earlier, we have referred to "sociological fashions." The phenomenon is real, but it would be an error to believe it to be the fruit of simple personal preferences. Behind sociological fashions, however much they may appear to be gratuitous, superficial, or simply bizarre, there is always an authentic interest, a group, a social class, which is structurally tied to it; a need for legitimation or manipulation; the exercise of a social power that cannot openly declare itself and that needs to mystify or conceal itself in order to guarantee its credibility and perpetuation. Sociological fashion is a symptom. The error lies in believing it to be the result of a strictly scientific calculation, whereas in actuality it represents an ideological choice, the consequence of the principle of personal, not abstractly free, preference; and, on the contrary, one strongly linked to a web of profound social interests—even if at times, in the individual researcher, these are unconscious. In any case, someone who would wait for his own subjects of research to come from the marketplace was inconceivable to Weber. We have already said that a large part of his comments and contributions were written to order, but this should not mislead us. The opportuneness of Weber's writings does not point to any propensity for bending to the everyday, to what was currently in vogue. Rather, it demonstrates a characteristically Weberian atittude: to take off from the everyday, from the analysis of the contingent problem, one that is circumscribed, in order to interpret it so that it is framed in a global vision: empirical material in a typological gallery in which news makes history. In this, Weber never lets himself down. He has not given us a *tractatus* of methodology, just as he has not given us a general sociology explicitly laid out according to an organic project individuated in all its parts. A work like that of Talcott Parsons's *The Social System*,[5] would not only not have been written by Weber, but would have seemed to him—if not simply a waste of time—a simple preparatory exercise, a way —apart from being a mistaken way—of beginning. (He would have seen it as a mistaken way because it circulates in the void, and does not hinge on a specific historical problem). In Weber there was no systematic ambition, no academic boasting. Weber worked with the patience, the experimental sense, and the taste for inventive improvisation of the intellectual craftsman. This is clear. The problem with which he grappled always seemed to him more important than his own personal "production." One might say that he liberates himself from his writings.

5. The Sociologist Needs Historical Culture

I am well aware of two hostile objections: first, the conditions of sociological research that prevail today in all industrially and technically advanced societies no longer permit sociologists to use the methods of artisans and individual laborers. Second, no contemporary sociologists have Weber's historical culture, culture that allowed him to place every single problem in its individual framework and in the global framework of which it was a part.

It is true that Weber belonged to the age of the *grands individus* and that from that point of view he is wholly nineteenth century, like Marx, like Saint-Simon, like Comte, and also like Durkheim, even if the brood of Durkheimians—Marcel Mauss, Maurice Halbwachs, etc.—to some extent modified the loneliness of the great artisan. There is a passage in Weber, in his work *Die Verhaltnisse der Landarbeiter im ostelbischen Deutschland ("The Conditions of Rural Labor in Germany East of the Elbe")*[6] in which, discussing the burning desire for liberty and for a life less restricted and richer in alternatives, which is basic to peasant emigration, there emerges with painful clarity the existential dimension of the work of the private scholar, alone in his study, immersed in the shadows that are scarcely dispelled by the light on his desk: "In the obscure, half-conscious thrust towards far-away countries, there is hidden a moment of primitive idealism. Whoever is unable to decipher this is unaware of the attraction of freedom. In fact, rarely does its spirit touch the quiet of our study."

There is no doubt but that the conditions of sociological research have been, from the technical point of view, profoundly changed. There is no student who is capable on his own of administering hundreds, sometimes even thousands, of questionnaires, and then collecting and making a systematic examination of them, and thence proceeding to the calculation of percentages and correlations (that is, correlations between the various replies; for example, how many answer in a given way to such a question as, "Do you like going to concerts?", have a particular academic qualification or particular social origin or specific job or income, and so on). One must add to this the imperative of an interdisciplinary or multidisciplinary standpoint for the research. Aside from the possibility of dealing globally and in a coordinated manner with the social phenomenon to be studied, and thus on the basis of planned collaboration with the urban planner, the historian, the economist, the geographer, the psychologist, the cultural anthropologist, and naturally ultimately, the sociologist, one has from the outset and in the course of research to resolve the really technical problems that require the help of specialists. How can one choose, for example, a representative sample of a given universe, without the expert opinion of a statistician who has specialized in this particular sector of statistical science?

And yet teamwork, however necessary, is not without its handicaps. I mention one among many—there is the tendency to bureaucratize scientific work, to make it a problem of simple financial investment. This means the prevalence of what I call the "herd instinct." When a problem "moves," it is for some reason which in any case no one seems to have previously had the time or interest to explore; according to the order of the day, everyone seizes upon it and it becomes photogenic and is transformed into a fashion. When this fashion has been exhausted, quite independently from the results achieved, one throws oneself once more into a moving group conformism and an undefeatable solidarity of interests in another direction, toward another problem, which probably has nothing to do with the one that preceded it. Financial worries, much more than those connected with the discovery of truth, become dominant. The question of the double role appears. The research scholar tends to divide between the scientist and the administrator. The two roles are contradictory; thus neurosis develops; paralysis versus aggressiveness. The most serious problem for the researcher becomes the way in which to keep the research group united and adequately coordinated. The interdisciplinary attitude is mythologized: a rigid application of the principle of division of labor to scientific research produces misunderstandings, compartmentalization, an unconscious duplication of errors, fierce rivalries between one section and another. In particular, this makes it impossible to obtain the multiplier effects of dialectical confrontation, of cooperation and reciprocal cross-fertilization. Organizational requirements prevail over scientific ones. The need for financial support leads to conformism, and discourages or tends to postpone projects that which, although they may be splendid, run the risk of not pleasing administrators. One opts for a specialism which, if it is not serious, is at least not understood or is hard to evaluate. One thus begins, little by little, to conceive of research and to evaluate it in terms of business efficiency, as though one were dealing with a commercial enterprise to be judged on the basis of the quantity produced; at the same time one finds oneself forced to lose sight of the universal sense of the problem; one falls into fragmentation, and gratuitousness. Sociological research thus becomes more and more technically impeccable and humanly—socially and politically—irrelevant. This is technical mastery without an aim. It is not surprising that financing ends up by being considered more important than ideas. In this sense a certain return to the artisan spirit is healthy, and Weber's example in this respect, also, has lost little of its impact.

To have, and in practice to make use, however, of one's own autonomy in the choice of research subjects means to have an extraordinary problematic awareness, a gift that does not drop from the skies; it necessarily presupposes a knowledge of historical culture far above the average. Max Weber had indeed an exceptional historical culture, a rare gift among sociologists, whether classic or contemporary. Let us leave aside the famous anecdote which sees him blessed as the best young historian and disciple in Germany by Mommsen, the great man in person, as soon as he had finished discussing his undergraduate thesis. The fact is that Max Weber was no amatuer historian. It is not necessary to refer to the loving *Lebensbild* written by his wife, Marianne, to be aware of the breadth and precision of his knowledge: from law to economics, from the evolution of the figurative arts to ethical systems, insofar as they influence and are conditioned by economic behavior, to politics as a vocation but also as a totality of procedures and techniques whereby power is effectively exercised. The multiplicity of Weber's interests was so rich and so broad as to make one think of him as a Renaissance man.

Indeed, this is not a question (as one might think on the basis of some pages written by his wife) of an encyclopedic mishmash, basically intellectually irresponsible. Weber's problematic awareness is so alert and so intense that everything—from religion to music, from history to law, from economics to anthropology—becomes usable material, and is actively fused together in the context of questions that are basic to it and that make up its deeper justification, over and above any seeming immediacy of his research. It did not matter to what argument he dedicated himself, with his usual acuity and passion; it might be the stock exchange or the conditions of the profession of journalist, the questions concerning the destiny of reason, the social significance of science, the possibility of a transition from formal rationality to essential rationality, or to the real reasons why men obey. These are the real problems to which all the other questions are connected, gathered together in clusters. These questions arise in Weber and return with the exceptional clarity that is connected with his profound historical culture. There is no contemporary sociologist who has a serious or even comparable knowledge of historical culture. Perhaps one might make an exception of Reinhard Bendix, but the average sociologist is as ignorant of history as he is informed in specific techniques of inquiry. He knows IBM machines better than archival documents. He also may well know how to program a computer, but there is no use asking him overly subtle questions concerning the major intellectual currents or social movements whose heritage we are still wearily traversing.

It is easy to understand all this, even to excuse it, but it should not be forgotten. The lack, the pure and simple forgetfulness, of the historical dimension in studies by contemporary sociologists—especially North American ones—is an obvious feature, and in any case so normal that it seems almost illegitimate to underline it. The classics of sociology certainly knew history and correctly evaluated its importance for the purposes of their research, but their historical sensitivity does not seem to have been sufficient. The influence of positivism, as a doctrine and as a mode of research, produced in this respect negative effects. Auguste Comte did not have the sense of individual, historically determinate societies. Historical peculiarities seemed to him accidents that could be neglected; his purpose was the construction of a "social physics" which in all respects rivals natural physics and the exact sciences. It also is to be noted that we are still concerned with the concept of science as the dispenser of a total, "divine" knowledge which is not probabilistic but dogmatic, not problematic but absolute, a knowledge on which Comte hung the whole future of humanity. This is because Comte spoke in the name of *humanité*. We must, however, be careful: this is a *humanité* that not only coincides with Western Europe but in fact with France. It is a case of unconscious Eurocentrism which is rather emblematic.

Herbert Spencer was much more cautious; he distrusted abstract, universalizing reasoning. He looked with the circumspect, differentiating attention of the trueborn empirical researcher at national and local realities with their singular and irreducible peculiarities, rooted in nonrepeatable historical evolutions. He lacked, however, the sense of historical development: his evolutionism is wholly based on biology, Darwinianism, and the diachronic movement of societies responds basically to a mainspring of blind, merely cumulative causation. His manner of working was that of a meticulous cataloguer, but one who was essentially mechanistic, for whom currents and basic historically determining events are calmly placed to one side and equated with transitory and irrelevant phenomena.

Emile Durkheim himself does not on close scrutiny escape the circle of positivism. His "specificity of the social," while it worthily saves sociological research from the univerifiable generalities of his predecessors, does not therefore become open to the understanding of determinate historical situations, of "happenings." Rather, we are still looking for a general law, a logical explanatory construct which in its tendency is metahistorical and untemporal. The very ontologization of "collective images" was, for Durkheim, the symptom of a tendency, never wholly overcome, to hypostasize determinate realities, contradictorily excluding them from the flow of history in the very moment in which he declares the specificity of their nature.

It is clear that between sociology and history there are wide differences. The historian works in the archives; the sociologist works—or should work—in the streets. The historian in the archives is concerned with history which is already past, while the sociologist does not reject daily news; indeed he finds in it—still in the warm, fluid state, with everything that is fragmented and fleeting, which accompanies everydayness—his basic raw material. It is useless to conceal this: to be a sociologist in a serious sense is an inconvenient profession. Historical knowledge, however—indeed, historical culture in the sense of totality of noneclectic, nonmiscellaneous knowledges—that is, historical culture as the totality of knowledge, plus a deep awareness—is basic for the sociologist. In order to give him the sense of perspective, a means of trying to connect basic empirical data with global meaning of the phenomenon so as not to allow him to forget, in favor of small pieces of research—even abundantly paid by little businessmen who commission them and are avid for any results in the shortest possible time—the important question is: where do we come from, where are we now, where are we going? Sociological explanation is different from historical explanation. History and sociology have in common their object of research: man living in society; man, as social being, and his institutions. The structure of sociological explanation is, however, conditional, tendentially standardized, typical, whereas that of historical explanation is causal and defining. For example, let us take the French Revolution: the historian tries to establish its precedents, delves into the archives to bring to light the relevant documents and evidence, determines the connections and empirical data of this historically determined situation. These are the empriical materials and interpretations that are most useful also to the sociologist. The questions that the latter asks, however, go beyond the specific, circumscribed phenomenon of the French Revolution as such, and may be formulated in the following terms: In what conditions (economic, social, political, cultural) does a revolutionary process take place; that is, a violent break with the existing social order? In other words, what are the socioeconomic and cultural conditions which pertain to the revolutionary phenomenon, which make possible and probable the coming-about of a revolution, empirically verifiable on the historical level? The reply to this question no longer refers only to the specific fact of a historically determinate revolution: it contains, rather, the elements for the construction of the abstract scheme or model (the framework) or, to use Weber's formula, "an ideal type," which acts as a term of reference and as a guide in the systematic gathering of empirical data, and in which different revolutions, essentially having taken place at the level of past and present historical experience, can be included, from the French to the Soviet revolutions, from the Spartacus rising to the Cuban and Chinese revolutions, and so forth (see, for a brief description of my present position in this regard, the recently published book *Storia e storie di vita*, Laterza, Bari, 1981).

In order to construct this model or "ideal-typical" scheme, it is clear that historical culture is an essential prerequisite. Sociology has, from its beginnings, experienced to the utmost, however, the temptation of seeking to arrive at an absolute scientific knowledge, able to formulate "laws" in a rigorous and dogmatic sense: laws that are universally valid, necessary and necessitating, and that are by definition insensitive to historical variability. Sociology has, from its beginnings, experienced the fascination —in reality more magical than scientific —of a knowledge that is not so much scientific as scientistic and timeless—the attraction, that is, of propositions and "laws" which are eternal and metahistorical. This has been true from the time of Comte. Supplied with a historical culture perhaps greater than is commonly believed, Comte was so obsessed with the idea of bringing order ("order and progress") into the chaos provoked by revolution as to turn the scientific rules of positivism—of which, not by chance, he ended up by believing himself to be the *grand prêtre*—into a dogmatic, absolute, all-encompassing message: in a word, a religious one.

6. Beyond Historicism and Positivism

It is in this perspective that we can understand why Max Weber did not intend, and obviously refused, to construct a "system," because he knew that this involved a contradictory and thus despairing undertaking. The idea of being able to find and formulate sociological generalizations that might be valid for all humanity—that is, for society in general—cutting them off from any specific historical background, and that despite this, they should not be reduced to mere tautologies or banal truisms, presupposes a totally standardized and homogeneous humanity: at most, this presupposes the interruption and blockage of historical development. In this sense, the fact that sociologies should still be basically tied to various differentiated national realities should not be understood as a symptom of immaturity or backwardness in the discipline. It is something deeper and more significant. This is a fact which helps us to remember that sociological concepts are not metahistorical, that they are instrumental in regards the historically mature problems of specific contexts, and that only within a determinate historical horizon can sociological research hope to redeem itself from gratuitousness and arrive at the fullness of its scientific significance and social function. The basic importance of Weber is precisely determined by the fact that he leaps into the heart of the problematic tension that exists between positivism and historicism — that is, between the tendency to consider human facts, which are always historical facts, as purely material realities, "factual" (*comme des choses,* as Durkheim says), whose understanding means the same thing as counting and measuring them (understanding as precision); and the contrary tendency that sees in the human fact something ineffable, nonstandardizable, an actual reality, something intimate and mysterious, that one can only "relive" and personally experience, but cannot in a positive manner analyze in such a way as to arrive at a knowledge and a public explanation—that is to say, one that is intersubjective and in all respects controllable. Max Weber goes beyond positivism and historicism. The limits of strictly positivistic sociology seem to have been for him absolutely clear. There is nothing surprising about that fact. Positivism had never really rooted itself in German culture, which was saturated in idealism and romantic spiritualism. Elsewhere, in Italy, for example, positivism was philosophically beaten and ultimately eliminated in the first years of this century, even before it had reached maturity and could provide the positive results of which it was undoubtedly the bearer, in regard to an Italian culture so inclined toward rhetoric. The value of positivistic sociology, even of the Comtian type—that is, of positivistic sociology in its most orthodox forms—is beyond question. Certainly, one can easily smile today at some of Comte's findings and at his religious reforms in general: the new calendar with the names of philosophers and scientists as a replacement for those of the traditional saints; the cult of Clothilde de Vaux, which too often openly points to the maniacal obsession of a man who was already ill and suffering; and so forth. The merit of positivism, especially of positivist sociologists, is clear. It won whole fields of human behavior and basic social institutions from the control—or, more precisely, the dead hand—of theological authority by relating them once more, against tradition and revelation, to ascertainable facts in their empirical related determinateness as well as to rational inquiry about them as social facts.

The specificity of the social, which was recovered by Durkheim from the path of Comtian tradition, was a permanent acquisition for the social sciences. Secondly, there is no sociological proposition which deserves serious consideration that does not have its empirical "price," or cannot refer back to its "accounts." These basic arguments are present—indeed, most solidly expressed—in Comte. The backward-looking polemics, which, especially in Italy, were fed by neoidealists and also by Marxists—the two positions, given their common framework, being so close, however, as to coincide—were not sufficient to remove this fact.

That Delio Cantimori, among others, recognized that at the origins of sociology there are reflections on the history of mankind and the attempt to define the concept of "society" as against the natural law and contractual ideas, thereafter adding that "Comte's was a deformation of the original, revolutionary and critical outlook (utopian) of Saint-Simon," should not surprise us.[7] Cantimori simply echoes Marx and Engels's famous judgment on Kant, in which they confine themselves to considering him the "natural son" of the gifted Saint-Simon.

Here, however, the lack of understanding seems so gross as to border on prejudice. The contribution of Kant's positivist questioning, even from a point of view internal to the rise of sociology as a science, is neither a marginal fact nor a simple "deformation" of *Saint-Simonisme,* which in any case Kant must have known at first hand. Since the time at which the different empirical sciences were progressively "freed" from the tutelage of philosophy, as I have noted elsewhere,[8] the aspiration toward a reunification and synthesis of the branches of human knowledge has had a role in the thought of scientists and philosophers. It has often been a matter of a mere dream or a pretext for verbal dialectical exercises. In Auguste Comte, however, this vague aspiration was changed into a fundamental requirement and an instrument of the first order for understanding and at the same time for modifying society.

Comte's starting point lay in the act of bringing out the fact that the various physical and social sciences of his time were not animated by the same *esprit.* Today we would say that they were understood as ontologically and methodologically divided into two major currents. On the one hand, there was the science of nature, the physical, natural world, essentially reduced to a unity by mechanistic Galileian and Cartesian outlooks, and in whose context research into "prime causes" was rejected in favor of limiting oneself to identifying and setting out the laws of phenomena by systematic observation. On the other hand, there were the historical and social sciences, which attempted to explain natural laws instead of first limiting themselves to establishing what they were. The basic problem—a problem which we shall see predominantly reemerging in the work of Weber—thus lay in introducing a unity of method into the system of the sciences. Comte maintains a definitive overcoming of the dichotomy between the positive method of the physiconatural sciences and the speculative method still used by the social sciences. Once one has discarded the hypothesis of the reconcilability of the two methods, and forcefully rejected the insufficiency, not to say the regressive nature, of the theologicometaphysical method, Comte fights for the extension and logical application of positive method in all fields of what is humanly knowable: for all sciences, be they of "nature" or of "spirit," to use this traditional, approximate terminology. What seems worth underlining is that this methodological struggle is not seen and maintained by Comte as a purely intellectual one. As against the polemical observations of Delio Cantimori, which have been in due course appropriated by other Marxist scholars so as to find a new and suggestive expression, latterly in Herbert Marcuse, one must remember that Comte's methodological considerations and his scientific work were only presented as a preliminary proposal, necessary but not exhaustive, and still less self-justifying, for a grandiose work of social, political, and moral renewal. One would not fully understand the *Cours de philosophie positive* without having constantly in front of one the *Système de politique positive*. In this sense, the interpretation, still recently popularized by Marcuse and Adorno, of a positivistic sociology—as though one were dealing with a sociology of resignation and passive acceptance of the *status quo*—seems untenable.

7. Sociology Is Not Social Physics

In regard to positivistic methodology, and the innumerable disciples of Comte and Spencer, Weber's position is more cautious and less sectarian. There is no difficulty in recognizing its values. Brought up in a culture that, with exemplary logic, denied a role and autonomous function to sociology as a science, relegating it, and at the most recognizing an auxiliary position for it, in regard to phenomena identified and analyzed on the level of and with instruments of historiography, Weber did not hesitate to involve himself to the ultimate in the theoretical and methodological foundation of the autonomy of the sociological judgment in the direction already opened up by the work of Ferdinand Toennies, but nonetheless with an undoubted originality. There is indeed no mystery that in his first works he concerns himself with field research according to a mode of investigation and a rigorous empirical observation based much more on statistical inquiry than on deductions of a speculative nature. This did not escape the attention of Ernesto Sestan, although Sestan, while taking part in the prevalent attitude toward sociology, is well aware of the qualitative distinction between a broadly historiographic inquiry and a sociological one. Sestan quotes Martin Offenbacher's study *Konfession und soziale Schichtung*[9] *(Religion and Social Stratification)*, 1901, in order to note that "Offenbacher, a pupil of Weber, was led into this type of research precisely by Weber." He adds, "However, in reality, these enquiries by Offenbacher are of a statistical nature, applied to the phenomenon of religion, and are in no way different, qualitatively and methodologically, from those which Weber himself had conducted in the first phase of his activity: especially as regards those on the agrarian conditions to the east of the Elbe."[10] Can we, however, state this sensitiveness in regard to the concrete and the circumscribed, this tendency for Weber to keep in mind the empirical data, not to fall into pure, unverifiable speculation: can we claim that this is really only characteristic of the first phase of his activity, or even, as Sestan suspects, is a simple derivation from the fact that Weber is not a "philosophical mind"? As we have noted above, there is reason to emphasize the theoretically important fact that Weber's methodological reflection never went around and around or forward in a void—it was always *a reflection on work in progress:* that is, it went forward by developing and constructing in the course of the actual research process, in the daily attempt to clarify its presuppositions, its direction, its meaning and instruments. Weber's opposition to positivistic methodology has in this sense little to do with the critique of the historical school concerned with preserving for historiography a position and a function which are dominant in regard to the other social sciences and in particular in regard to sociology. What Weber rejects in positivistic methodology seems naturally close to the critical questions posed by German historicist culture against positivism: (1) the immediate, ingenuous objectivism, that is to say the pure and simple abolition of the gnoseological problem, even if Weber himself tends to resolve within methodological discussions and in terms of pure method the knotty problem of the theory of knowledge, distancing himself in this regard clearly from his philosophical mentors (Windelband and Rickert); (2) the Comtian postulate of society as an absolute rational whole, dominated by a totality of iron immutable laws whose discovery and formulation should be the task of sociology, a preeminent preliminary task that is necessary if there is to be any plan of social reform and that confers on sociology a primacy with regard to all other natural and social sciences, by making it the real queen of social sciences. Weber thus rejects in the last analysis—and in complete agreement in this respect with German historicism—the equivalence that Comte sought to establish between physics and sociology, between the physical sciences and what Durkheim called the "physique des moeurs." Nevertheless, with equal vigor and an abundance of unanswerable, detailed argument, Weber likewise criticizes the traditional assumptions of German historical culture, which was the cultural ground of his origin.

8. Values Depend Upon Individual Choice

Weber not only does not accept the equivalence between physics and sociology expressed by Comte and by the positivists in general—an equivalence that amounts to the hasty negation of history—he also attacks the counterposing, set out in theoretical form by Dilthey, between the sciences of the human spirit (the historical sciences and social sciences, including psychology) and the sciences of nature. This hinges on the principle that man is able to understand his historical and social experience insofar as he can relive it as an internal mental experience, though this is not possible—and not even significant or desirable—in the natural physical sciences. Second, Weber distances himself also from Windelband and Rickert, for whom the validity of the historical and social sciences—or as Weber would often say, "Sciences of culture"—must be sought not within them in the manner in which they proceeded to construct their own logical explanatory schemas, but rather in the relation to the values that they refer to as supreme selective criteria in respect to the gathering and systematic interpretation of empirical data. It is these values for Windelband and Rickert, their absolute and extramundane character in a real metaphysical sense, that confer validity and meaning on sociological research; whereas for Weber this validity and meaning cannot depend on any metaphysical "value-relation." It is, on the contrary to be sought within the very process of research, so that understanding of the meaning of the phenomena does not refer to the metaphysical value that is held to underwrite it, but depends rather on the capacity of the researchers empirically to discover and determine the basic conditions that are responsible for making true on the historical plane the phenomenon grasped in its specific individuality. In other words, values—the "commanding criteria" of the research—are for Weber no longer universal and necessary absolutes. Rather, they are in themselves the results of choice: they reflect the dispositions and the interest of the researcher and are linked to his orientation, his existential predilections. This argument is necessarily complex, and reflects a difficult process of mediation which in Weber does not always find clear expression. It would seem ungenerous, however, to suspect when faced with the objectively difficult nature of the problems in question that this complexity has an autobiographical rather than a theoretical origin. "No longer merely statistics, nor only an elaboration of patiently gathered data, according to the schemas of normal economic science. It is impossible to follow him in the tortuous meanderings of the nervous crisis which afflicted him for more than five years.... The taste for clear precision of concepts in handling his discipline Weber had, indeed, always had. However, now the native tendency became more acute: the distance from the professorial chair and the obligations connected with it—preparation of courses, exams, lessons, seminars, etc.—gave him the pleasure of abandoning himself to spiritual wanderings without a precise aim; to deepen, to leave off, to take up again, to defer, what he had earlier necessarily had to finish with because of the professional needs which could not be neglected or put off. Now there was time: he could spend long hours in the external inertia imposed on him by the treatment for his illness, looking for the logical presuppositions of his discipline. But this mental labor, connected with a still too slender thread to a possible eventual application to the concrete, was bound to make his illness worse, rather than to soothe it: so one may suppose."[11]

Sestan's surmises raise a serious problem that unfortunately cannot be investigated to the full in this present work. By themselves these surmises are seriously reductive of the significance of Weber—not to say defamatory. The problem is, however, a real problem, perhaps more in Weber's case than for others devoted to the social sciences. Indeed, the nterpenetration between intellectual life and biographical matters is closer and perhaps more decisive, and the cause of more suffering, for him than for others. It is enough to think of his attraction/repulsion to a political career, his ambiguity toward power, and the ethical implications this involved. Max Weber is certainly an inconvenient character to decipher, but it seems scarcely acceptable to get rid of him with gossip. The portrait of him left to us after his death by his widow does not help a great deal in this regard. Inevitably, it is a partisan portrait; it falls into emotive hagiography. There is no doubt, on the other hand, that Weber's being inconvenient derives from the basically contradictory character of his existential experience and biographical makeup, a character that is reflected with great precision in the asystematic path of his work.

It might seem important to establish beyond family and academic gossip the origins of the contradictory nature of Max Weber's character, which is in many aspects so strong and determined. It seems clear that we are dealing with a schizoid personality, inwardly controlled by many—even too many—"vocations." If we accept the definition of neurosis as a state of painful paralysis determined by the force of two simultaneous opposing tendencies, Weber seems to be a typical neurotic. Even from a simple, textual analysis of his work, it is clear that within him there coexist and struggle a very strong political temperament and an irrevocable need for intellectual clarity. Perhaps—indeed, certainly—the roots of Weber's obscure illness go deeper. The attempts to psychoanalyze the illustrious dead, as we know, have not generally met with much success. The attempt concerning President of the United States Woodrow Wilson, which tends to demonstrate the connection between his psychic blocks and the narrow, Calvinist, moral rigor that he demonstrated at the Versailles Peace Conference after the First World War, certainly did not lead to conclusive results. The analysis of a preeminently psychoanalytical kind to which David Reisman subjected the work and more generally the scientific position of Thorstein Veblen cannot be considered any more satisfactory.

Weber's case would presumably be even more difficult. One would, in addition, need to have detailed reliable information about his relations with his wife, Marianne, and even more about those with his mother, just as the relationship with his father, which we know to have been generally dramatic, would have to be clarified—relations that reached a crisis point following the decision of the wife to visit the son, Weber, who was already married. Furthermore, one would need to establish what truth there is in the insistent rumor concerning Weber's impotence. What should never be forgotten, however, in the course of this whole, complex analytical operation is the limitations to which psychological and psychoanalytical explanations of this kind are exposed: explanations based on reconstructions that are *a posteriori,* without the benefit of a direct confrontation. This is not all; it should likewise never be forgotten that the exceptional nature and greatness of Weber, like that of Thorstein Veblen and others, become evident precisely through the ability to transcend in certain important aspects the facts of his own familial and social origins. The psychological significance, as a significant part of the causal matrix of personality attitudes, has its necessary function, which is, however, far from being sufficient and further still from being exclusive. One should beware of making an acritical use of it as a specialist is, nonetheless, tempted to do. One might well extract from it a misleading skeleton key, by means of which one might mechanically explain everything and nothing at one and the same time.

9. In Defense of the Individual, even at the risk of irrationalism

Whether it is more or less directly related to the years of Weber's nervous breakdown and his forced inactivity, what one can state is that his complex methodological meditation moves toward, and ultimately flows into, the most mature current of contemporary scientific thought: (1) research instruments have to be refined and adjusted in the course of the research itself; (2) there is no break between the sciences of the mind and sciences of nature; there is no intuitionism and no objectivism, but rather a purely methodological distinction; (3) the "ideal type" as an instrument used by sociology to achieve its own ends, which consists in analysis and understanding of real human behavior by individual agents rationally directed toward an end and referring to the attitude of others; (4) hence, this means the unity of the sciences in the search for "uniformities" or probabilistic tendencies: these are no longer dogmatic "laws" in the sense of ingenuous positivism; (5) we are dealing with uniformities which for sociology are constructed from human action as action provided with meaning, and these are expressed in "ideal types" which, contrary to the generalizations of the physical sciences—which are seeking to reorder a multiplicity of phenomena—aim at *explaining phenomena in their specific individuality.* Weber's aim is purely individualistic: *for him, individual action is the atom from which all sociological research should begin.*

The counterposing of Weber's outlook and the Marxist one at this point can leave no room for doubts. What one must stress, rather, is the contradiction between this methodological aim, to which Weber was always to be explicitly, if not absolutely emphatically, faithful, and his concrete research work in which he always chose as themes for investigation *structural* ones, great historical subjects like capitalism or world religions, and from which he never slipped save occasionally, and then more from the point of view of professional language than that of basic concepts on the psychologistic or purely interindividual level. This contradiction is an invaluable guide to the limits of all Weber's work, his inability and refusal to create a link between the intellectual clarity of knowledge and understanding, on the one hand, and practicopolitical decision on the other, so that the lucidity of the analysis should be transformed into action and political force.

The obstacle here is represented by the personal choice of Weber, not by logical impossibility. This crucial point has been grasped with great insight: "Weber's methodological individualism—"unthinkable" if it is referred to his *structural analyses of institutional orders and spheres* . . . becomes 'understandable' only if referred to *his* special concern, which is rooted in a 'value judgment' rather than being based on a 'relation to values.' Trying to redeem the liberty of man, his choices and his 'reason,' Weber ends up by understanding the latter as 'rationality' (both formal and technical), in which the totality of social relations is only a simple datum to give shape to the content, meaning for individual concrete actions. The weakness of this methodological position, (which Weber himself abandoned in the course of two analyses) is scarcely concealed by his formal, defining rigor. His kind of methodological materialism ('real men,' 'concrete actions,' 'sensible activity') rather than pushing him towards the consideration of the structure of social condition (and of relations of conditioning)—apart from the implicit importance that he gives in the heuristic, ideal-typical construct, and rather in relation to the growth and expansion of individual motivtations—leads him instead towards a societal nominalism which has no exit: this is almost a supposition that man and his interests and individual motives had their justification in these elements themselves."[12]

Weber therefore studied—chose to study—*structure*. He obstinately refused, however, to recognize in it the determining weight in the causal explanation of human behavior. He feared, to put it simply, that this would end up by flattening the world of free, individual volitions, that the "realm of ideas" would thus be endangered and that the force of basic economic relations would ultimately be seen to be decisive for the whole of social development. Marx—the familiar Banquo's ghost who obsessed Weber all his life—returns as the main interlocutor. What if Marx was right? What if the economic structure really alone or as a basic *prius*, were to be the decisive force in the totality of forces and interests and values that make up and mark social development with its dynamic impulse? What would then happen to the realm of ideas? What would happen to individual liberties?

10. Science Clarifies the "Cost" of Choices, but in regard to the choices themselves it has nothing to say.

At the end of his long, tormented meditation, Weber was above all concerned to redeem the possibility of the choice of the individual. Because of this basic reason he refused to establish a necessary connection between intellectual clarity and practical decision; that is, between theory and practice. He wanted to preserve the possibility of choice for the individual between various conflicting "points of view." He wanted to maintain intact the individual's autonomy of judgment, free to choose as an alternative what, independently of the result of the research, he might retain for himself to be more useful; he scented in Marxism the trap of a unilateral explanation that might claim to make itself pass for a total, exhaustive explanation. The validity of an aim, of an end, cannot be guaranteed by science. It cannot be demonstrated in an intersubjective sense as though it were endowed with a collectively dominant value: the beginning and end of a social action is still the individual will, which no scientific calculation can guarantee, and standardize, free from uncertainty and from the risk which surrounds it.

What, therefore, can we expect from science according to Weber? Not much. We certainly cannot expect to find recipes for the "correct life": we cannot expect from it a recipe in which we might find higher values to follow, and those which on the contrary should be fought against. Weber's warning contains a radical, cutting critique in regard both to romantic intuitionism and also scientistic claims. Weber says, "Let whoever wants a 'vision' go to the cinema . . . And I should like to add: Whoever wants prophecy should go to a monastery. The discussion regarding the relation of value which exists between the civilizations dealt with here is not even touched upon by a word. Yet it is true that the course of human events, for whosoever looks at an epoch, is disturbing. However, one would do best to keep to oneself one's own little personal comments, as one also does in front of the sea and the mountains—at least so long as one doesn't feel called to and capable of artistic creation or a prophetic mission."[13] Again, "An empirical science can never teach anyone what he should do, but only what he can do—and—in determinate circumstances—what he wants.... To make a judgment of the validity of these values is, however, a question of faith and possible in addition a task of speculative concern and interpretation of life and the world as regards their meaning: but it is certainly not the object of an empirical science in the meaning adopted in these pages." [4]

Thus Weber. If, however, science cannot tell us what is the "correct life," if it cannot give us a unequivocal certain response to the questions, What shall we do? How should we live? What can it tell us? What is its social function? On the basis of what services to humanity can it justify itself?

Weber's response is very clear. The sciences of culture, and in the first place sociology, can tell us nothing definitive about the validity of values. Weber seems to think that this would be too convenient. In the great mass of values struggling among themselves in the confusion that the individual sees as the result of the "polytheism of values," sociology can, however, perform an important demystificatory function. It is capable of informing us in detail what means there are for looking at values, and further, for determining the conditions of their verification on the historical level. In other terms, if sociology cannot tell us what value is absolutely preferable as more valid, and leaves to the individual the burden and responsibility of choice, it nevertheless is capable of calculating the "cost" of this choice and of offering us thus elements of judgment to decide if the means at our disposition are sufficient and proportional to the aims we set ourselves. Sociology thus has a task of clarification, not a normative one but rather one might perhaps say one of "mental hygiene" in regard to the aims to which the individual aspires; that is, an essentially critical task, meta- and anti-ideologically tending to bring forward, through the adequacy of the available means regarding the end and the calculation of the consequences of an action, the minimal prerequisites for rationality of thought and action. For Weber, rationalism, and included in it that is sociology, is an instrument of liberation from psychosocial conditioning, through which the individual can arrive at pure rationality, even if this is only formal. In this sense, the ultimate result of Weberian thought involves a precise inversion of the position of Ferdinand Toennies, for whom *Gemeinschaft*, that is traditional community, made up the first fundamental value.

Far from, and foreign to, any romantic return to the original traditions, social reality for Weber presents itself as an infinite chaos of social and value conflicts, arising not from economic or class conflicts, but from those of temperament, ideas, generation, and style. There is no eschatological vision of a more or less long-term range that provides Weber with comfort. Rather, he foresees that once economic conflicts have been resolved there will be other conflicts regarding power and prerogative, tied to the ideological debate and to bureaucratic power, indifferent to any change in dominant ideologies. This is a Heraclitean vision, not without its grandeur, even though it is exposed to the temptation of irrationalism. What is Weber's own major weakness, the rejection of the link between theory and practice, his lack of political decisiveness, the fact that he was never able to complete the "intellectual sacrifice" that every political decision and every ideological militancy involve, is changed by Weber the sociologist into an attitude that is so disinterested and open that it allows him a special power and breadth of analysis.[15]

CHAPTER TWO

ETHICAL NORMS AND ECONOMIC BEHAVIOR

1. Interested Misunderstandings

A writer's fortune can involve tortuous paths and curious vicissitudes. For instance, the interest in the works of Vilfredo Pareto or Roberto Michels was born again in Italy as a result of a rebound from the United States. Max Weber's reputation, in Europe and the Western world, is linked to two short essays; *The Protestant Ethic and the Spirit of Capitalism* (1904-1905) and *Protestant Sects and the Spirit of Capitalism* (1906). One must acknowledge that the reason for his unexpected reputation is at least in part spurious. It is difficult to imagine today two essays on economic history and sociohistoriographic interpretation unexpectedly becoming best sellers. The basic reason for the acclaim immediately bestowed on these two works of Weber's—over and beyond the argument that they contain and the skill of their author in demonstrating it—must certainly be traced to the intellectual climate and the philosophical, historiographical, and social-science environment of the period, which from time to time searched out authoritative contributions to use polemically against historical materialism in general and particularly against Marxism.

Once Weber's research had been published, what more could be asked? At least in a first cursory, if impartial, reading, the data, the interpretations and in fact all Weber's reasoning seemed to lend itself admirably to a toughly critical use in the face of the materialist interpretation of history and social development. Marx's position seemed to be capable of being simply overturned, turned inside out like a glove. Marx and Engels in all their major works, although in a concise manner in the *Manifesto,* had argued for the priority of the economic structure and material interests of life in determining ideologies, political, religious, and juridical systems; now here was an eminent German scholar coming to show that not only was it not the economy which produced religious and moral systems, but that instead it was ethical norms that determined, in an empirically demonstrable manner, economic life, the development of capitalism, its organization and "spirit."

It is clear that we are dealing, in regard to both Weber and Marxism, with grace misunderstandings and crude oversimplifications. Marx and Engels never mechanically counterposed economic structure, or *Unterbau,* to superstructural phenomena, or *Ueberbau,* by the latter—seen as secondary products and historically passive ones—derived from the former. It is also simply not true that Weber's problem consists in overturning this schema and that it would thus wear itself out in an anti-Marxist polemic. We have already said that it was very far from Weber's mind to set up and weigh system against system. Not only is this evident from the record, but his very methodology, his concrete way of working, excluded the possibility of constructing a complete, totally inclusive doctrinaire system, and in any case his critique of Marxism is not to be confused with vulgar anti-Marxism. In this regard, it is useful to remember how, when he intervened during the first congress of sociology in Frankfurt in 1910, Weber particularly concentrated on the deformations and misunderstandings of which Marxism was the victim, explicitly stating that historical materialism was misunderstood in such a crude way that if Marx were still living, he would be dumbfounded by it. [1]

2. The Reciprocal Conditioning of Ethics and Economics

An acritical reading of the Weberian text that is best known and most suggestive, *The Protestant Ethic and the Spirit of Capitalism,* is especially open to the dangers of a distorted interpretation. It is inevitable that one start from that. One must, however, be contextually aware both of Weber's frist field research—on peasants and conditions of agricultural work—which dates from 1896—and of the basic studies on the concept of "economic ethics" *(Wirtschaftsethik),* which date from 1917. Otherwise, one runs the risk of not understanding the way in which Weber saw the connection between ethical norms and economic behavior, between religion as a doctrine and as daily practice and the structure and orientation of social life. Above all, one risks deriving from this a profoundly impoverished conception, reduced to a mechanical formula, and failing to see in all its richness and problematic character, the reciprocal and bidirectional conditioning between ethics and economics, on which Weber never tired of insisting and of which he offered examples derived from five great world religions—Confucianism, Hinduism, Buddhism, Christianity, and Islam—to which, as Weber himself wrote, one must naturally add, "Judaism, both because it contains, for full understanding of the latter two world religions, decisive historical assumptions, and because of its particular historical significance, partly real and partly presumed, for the development of the modern economic ethic of the West."[2]

The earliest research done by Weber is useful in this respect. In fact, it clarifies how from the initial phases of his scientific work he never set out to look into absolute "essences," or to hunt for "prime causes" which were not caused, but rather went very cautiously into an inquiry on the basis of the modes that are typical of sociological reasoning, essentially comparative and synoptic. Weber worked with the clear intention of identifying and contrasting, by connecting them, the conditions of historically verifying phenomena, so as to bring out their possible and meaningful interconnections. For example, already in the first scientific work by Weber, *Roman Agrarian History and Its Significance for Public and Private Law,* whereby he obtained in 1890 his license to teach history, it was the declared intention of the author to analyze "with the experimental method" the interrelations between the specific forms and techniques of measuring plots of land and the public and private juridical relations of global society during the era of classical Rome. What is important in this first work is not so much the determination of the specific content of these forms, a determination that had been attempted and successfully achieved by innumerable historians and scholars of classical antiquity, as the discovery and determination of a relationship, that is a "meanful interconnection," between juridical norms and the technique of agrarian measurement.

It is this sense of the universal nature of social phenomena, this sensitivity to the type and forms of interaction of their component parts— the types and forms which from time to time must be established through empirical research—that really represents the basic, essential quality of sociological work. Even when Weber speaks and writes about the "spirit" of capitalism the form of words may seem to be, and in my own personal view undoubtedly is, unfortunate; the substance and method of procedure in the research, however, afford no room for doubt. Even in this case, Weber is not concerned with establishing the "spirit—that is, the essence" of capitalism—and defining it once and for all by boxing it up in a formal definition. Rather, he is concerned with grasping and analyzing the historical "conditions" in the broad sense—or the economic, political, cultural, and moral (religious) conditions—that are present in its development or that block and make impossible or difficult the development of that historical *individuum* which we call capitalism.

3. Basic Analytical Concepts

The purpose of Weberian analyses is thus never that of freezing the historical phenomenon—capitalism, feudalism, or Confucianism, for example—in a dogmatic definition. Rather, it lies in the attempt to demonstrate that everything is always in movement: that at the historical level there are no eternal essences, but only conditions which are by definition transient; that every historical analysis can only be an analysis of "a particular point of view" and that thus, of necessity, it forms part of a "global perspectivism," which makes problematic and relative the results achieved, by preventing their solidification into a dogma or into a naturalistic "law." There emerges clearly the importance of the intercultural comparative dimension (in the sense of cross-cultural) in Weber's analyses. Furthermore, this explains the paradoxical fact, recently once again more stressed, that the most important analytical concepts elaborated by Marx shine out very clearly if viewed in the light of extra-European research, such as research regarding non-Christian religious systems, even when they may have been elaborated and refer to European situations such as "Protestantism," "lay Catholicism" and "the spirit of capitalism."

In this sense it is important, before we move on to the exposition of the principal conclusions of Weber in regard to determinate historical phenomena, to consider briefly some analytical concepts that he frequently employed and that indeed make up the main headings of his theoretical conceptual apparatus, especially in the study of the relationship between ethical norms and economic behavior. Apart from the basic categories, which recur in all Weber's writings, such as (1) "social action" *(Soziale Handeln)*, which points to action directed toward the behavior of other specific individuals; (2) "social relation" *(Soziale Beziehung)*, which points instead to the possibility in reality that "social action" may be carried out whatever the basis on which this possibility rests, for example, friendship, love, competition, etc.; (3) "use" *(Brauch)*, "custom" *(Sitte)* and "fashion," which point to the repetition through time of social action and thus the rise of uniformities tied to factual habits (use), which in turn consolidate themselves (custom) and prepare the ground for habitual behavior which is not formally codified but is to a certain extent binding (fashion); (4) "community" *(Gemeinschaft)*, which consists of a social relationship based on the subjective sentiment of a "common belonging" *(Zusammengehörigkeit)*; (5) "association" *(Vergesellschaftung)*,[3] which on the other hand emphasizes the more correctly rational aspect, which is thus foreseeable and calculable, in social action—we shall here look at the Weberian concepts which directly concern our theme, and which I find synthetically laid out in the kind of summary of the *Religionssoziologie* which we find in the introduction, entitled "The Economic Ethics of World Religions," making a comparative study of the sociology of religion.

4. Economic Ethics

First, one must understand correctly what Weber had in mind when he used the formula "economic ethics." Many of Weber's critics—Carlo Antoni being among the most careful and famous of them—have complained that Weber's exposition of the theological texts and the doctrinal presuppositions of Protestant sects, for example, is inaccurate. From this delicately doctrinal deficiency, they derive a critical argument, which they believe to be fatal to Weber's thesis, according to which there should be a chain of necessity between Protestant ethics and the rise and development of capitalism. These critics, generally highly sophisticated students of theological texts and moral philosophy—that is to say, champions of speculative reasoning—are not aware, however, that when Weber uses the word "ethic" he always and only means *lived ethic;* that is to say, not the abstract moral rules logically systematized into a philosophy or a moral theology, but rather the moral rules as they are translated into average everyday behavior. For this reason, Benjamin Franklin's autobiography or Richard Baxter's *Book of Devotions* are more important to Weber than Calvin's *Institutes of the Christian Religion.* The critics are thus firing, with an abundance of doctrine, at a mistaken target. This is strange, because Weber in this respect is very clear: "What is taken into consideration is not the ethical theory of theological textbooks which serve only as a means of knowledge (in certain circumstances undoubtedly important), but the *practical impulses to action* established in the psychological and pragmatic connections of religions."[4]

One hardly needs to recall, however, that these "connections" do not, by themselves, form a necessary unidirectional linkage from ethics to economics. That the "point of view" adopted by Weber is that of one who is investigating the economic "weight" of the ethical-religious system does not mean that he was not conscious that the social phenomenon being studied was, like all social phenomena, a global reality whose explanation could not in any way be expressed in unilateral terms. Any interconnection established by way of empirical research is of value and always functions in two directions. From the studies in 1904, dealing with "capitalism," it is clear that for Weber "every attempt at explanation . . . given the basic importance of economics, ought above all to consider economic conditions, but the inverse causal relationship should not be left unobserved. For economic rationalism mainly depends, apart from on the rationality of technique and law, on the capacity and disposition of men to determine forms of practical, rational conduct in life. . . . To the most important elements which in all countries formed human conduct, belonged in the past magical and religious powers, and the ideas of duties strictly connected with such beliefs."[5]

What then is "economic ethics"? Logically, according to his general standpoint, Weber argues that every concrete example of economic ethics is the result of a "complicated formation," which is "conditioned in a very complex manner." Indeed, "no economic ethics has ever been conditioned only in a religious sense. . . . However, certainly one—better, only one—of the determinants of economic ethics is also the religious characterization of the conduct of life."[6] From this first definition of economic ethics by Weber, it is easy to grasp how we are here confronted with a broader perspective than that which characterizes his work on Protestantism and European capitalism. It is true that Weber undertook his research on extra-European and non-Christian religions with the aim of finding supplementary supporting material for his argument concerning the connection between Protestantism and capitalism in such a way as to be able to establish this link and its importance by demonstrating that where the Protestant ethic or some decisive element of it was absent, capitalism failed to take root and develop. One, however, must recognize the fact that the comparative studies on world religions enlarged the perspective of Weber beyond this objective. They did so, moreover, to the extent of no longer involving simply the problem of the relationship between Protestantism and capitalism, but the general problem itself of economic development in a rational direction in countries that were technically backward, as well as that of their political and institutional modernization.

As Samuel N. Eisenstadt has effectively pointed out in his essay, "Religione e mutamento sociale in Max Weber" (*La Critica sociologica*, no. 28, Winter 1973-74), the economic ethic does not point to specific religious injunctions concerning correct behavior in the economic field, nor is it a simple intellectual derivation or practical corollary of the intellectual contents of the theology or philosophy predominant in a given religion. Economic ethics, as one deduces above all from Weber's analysis of non-European religions, is concerned instead with a general model of "religious" or "ethical" orientation. In this orientation, there is contained the evaluation of a specific institutional sphere, based on the premises of a given religion or tradition in regard to the cosmic order and its relation with human and social existence, and consequently, with the organization of social life. One may thus conclude that economic ethics is, in a sense, a code, a general "formal" orientation, a "deep structure," which programs or regulates actual, concrete social organization.

However, Weber, Eisenstadt notes, contrary to many modern structuralists, did not understand this code as a purely "formal" means of organizing a simple series of symbolic, abstract contents. He saw it as the key to discovering the most important symbolic, structural, and organizational elements of human and social existence. Here, consequently, in the research on non-Christian and extra-European religions, the context significantly broadened: economic ethics crossed over from the properly economic sphere and involved society as a whole, leading to important distinctions between "the position of a stratum" and "class situation." It forced one to formulate concepts concerning "the ethics of status" and "political ethics"; that is to say, the religious evaluation of the political sphere, or of the various dimensions regarding status; and further forced one to distinguish, within "class situation," the different categories of "possessors of income" (landed proprietors, owners of men, state proprietors, owners of values) by subdividing them into "possessing classes" and "classes of profit," the latter being primarily conditioned by the market.

It is useful once more to recall in Weber's own words the concepts of "charisma" (a quality of personality transcending the everyday, not mattering if it be real, presumed, or supposed), and of "traditionalism" (spiritual adaptability and the faith in what is customary or agreed upon as an inviolable norm for action). It is also useful to recall the concept of "the power of the rule," or "formalistic, juridical rationalism," which is thus bureaucratic (the impersonal tie of the objective "duty of office" which, like "competency" is determined by rationally instituted norms in a manner so stable that the legitimacy of domination is transformed into the legality of the general rule). These concepts are defined and indeed demonstrated in the very act in which they are grasped through the analysis of concrete, historical situations, in the cited introduction to "comparative researches on the sociology of religion." There is no doubt, however, that Weber's analytical genius is shown fully and openly in his work on Protestantism and capitalism.

5. Capitalism as a Thirst for Gain Rationally Moderated

What is capitalism? Are we dealing with a typical and exclusive product of Western European civilization, or is capitalism also to be found in other civilizations endowed with different religious, political, and cultural systems? In trying to reply to these preliminary questions, Weber obviously overturned current opinion regarding capitalism and capitalists: starting from a position of common sense, he demonstrated all its inadequacy. Common sense and general opinion in the first instance see in capitalism the thirst for gain and wealth, the classic *auri sacra fames.* Weber notes in passing that this commonplace has at times also been blessed by the conviction of well-known scholars—as, for example, Werner Sombart. This attribution, however, is too universal to be of assistance in the definition of an economic phenomenon like capitalism. Weber observes that the thirst for money, the aspiration to acquire as much wealth as possible, "has in itself nothing in common with capitalism. This desire can be found amongst waiters, doctors, coachmen, artists, women of pleasure, corruptible employees, soldiers, bandits, amongst crusaders, gaming saloons and beggars." Weber's catalogue could go on forever. Let us note, however, that all societies are, to a greater or lesser extent, "acquisitive societies," to use R. H. Tawney's formula. The urge to acquire money, as Sombart says in his work *Modern Capitalism*, is a universal type of impulse.

What differentiates a given society and civilization from others is the mode of acquisition, the ways whereby the impulsion toward money finds its practical realizattion and satisfaction. Possibly Bertolt Brecht was right when he stated that between the founder and the robber of a bank there is no basic difference. The technical difference in their method of operation is, however, unquestionable. The great capitalists who began to dominate the social and political scene in the United States of America after the end of the Civil War are traditionally called "robber barons" —that is, robbers on a huge scale—but it is indisputable that between these captains of industry and the earlier pirates there were deep operational and motivational differences.

These differences can be summed up in two fundamental ways: (2) capitalism is identified with the tendency toward gain in a rational and continuous capitalist enterprise—to gain that is always renewable; that is, to profitability. Weber emphasizes that in a capitalist order, any single enterprise that did not concentrate on the possibility of achieving profitability would be condemned to perish. The pirate makes coups, and his gain is strictly occasional; but the capitalist is a capitalist to the extent to which he organizes his own enterprise on a continuous basis founded on rationally calculated expectations; (2) in contrast to the productive forms of classical antiquity and of other civilizations, both feudal and extra-European, the West, says Weber, has in the modern era introduced a type of capitalism that is quite different and that has never been developed elsewhere: the rational organization of formally free labor.

Thus, not only can capitalism not be identified with the thirst for gain and the irrational impulse toward acquiring money, but it is, indeed, exactly the opposite. It presupposes, and in every case requires for its development through time, the "rational" tempering of that impulse. As

Weber sums up his thought on this key point of his theory, he seems to grasp that the emphasis on the rational character and calculation of capitalist enterprises aids decisively to give the capitalist a portrait—perhaps undeservedly—photogenic. This argument has its price, however, which Weber seems prepared to pay by limiting himself to warning the reader that the rationality which he is discussing in connection with capitalism and capitalists is a purely technical or operational rationality. In other words, it is a rationality that excludes a basic value judgment and ends up by being identical with the power and capacity to serve one's own interests —that is, to exploit circumstances by turning them to one's own profit. "An economic capitalist action means for us," says Weber, "an act which rests on the expectation of gain derived from the easy exploitation of current situations of exchange, and thus from the probability of formally peaceful gain. Violent acquisition (formal and actual) follows its special laws, and it is not useful—if indeed one cannot prevent this from being done—to place it in the same category as activity directed according to the probabilities of gain through exchange."[8]

By rejecting open violence and constraint on a personal level (in contrast, note the slavery of classical antiquity and the glebe serfs in the feudal era), capitalism needs the moment of integration—impersonal, formally free—in which the relation between worker and employer appears as a free contract of a juridical nature, in which the competition between the enterprises that form the "market" develops. Here Weber touches on a crucial aspect and is well aware of it. For capitalism, freedom of negotiation is basic. The individual freedoms of the Enlightenment are revealed here, once the clouds of revolutionary enthusiasm and the idyll of the universalistic slogan of "liberty, equality, fraternity"—in their true, economically weighted social function—have blown away. The principle of individual formal freedom not only guarantees the right to the ownership of private property in the means of production; it guarantees the real possibility of acquisition and the possibility of movement in the market by way of the competitive struggle which, Weber notes, "formally" liberates, even if in reality—that is "materially"—the market is dominated by monopolies and cartel agreements between the major enterprises.

To say the least, the problem of the subaltern labor power is brilliantly resolved. Materially, the modern worker's life situation is identical to that of the classical slave; he is formally free to sell himself to the highest bidder as though his contractual power were equal to that of the possessing partner of capital. The capitalist thus achieves, at the real level of relations of force, an obvious advantage over the slave owner of classical antiquity, who was bound to look after his *famuli* as members of his family, living resources in the context of his domestic economy. Formal rationality is expressed in the juridical system of the West, which implies the functioning of an impersonal public administration and a "democratic" political institutional structure that tempers the rational impulse to make money by channeling it into the bureaucratic routine of the enterprise's productive and distributive procedures, temporally continuous and "scientifically" organized. It finds its support and ultimate justification in the principle of individual liberty that defines liberal,Western European civilization. This is the obvious product and also the masterpiece of the revolutionary struggle conducted by the bourgeoisie of the Enlightenment against the privileges of the aristocracy.

Weber feels himself a child of this bourgeoisie, tied to and educated in its ideals and vision of the world. The aspect of pathos in his work and personality derives from the fact that this son of the bourgeoisie cannot, for reasons of "intellectual honesty," close his eyes to its contradictions and the abyss that opens up between abstractly sanctioned rights and principles and the actual material conditions of life.

It is difficult, however, not to sense the echo of pride where Weber outlines, in *Economy and Society* and also in *The Protestant Ethic,* the "exclusively Western" characteristics of rationality in the capitalist enterprise, and when he asks himself rhetorically why this same development did not take place in China or in India. Weber, perhaps in an unconsciously triumphalistic tone, asserts: "Only the West knows rational capitalist enterprises with fixed capital, free labor, specialization and rational connection of labor, and division of functions in the framework of a pure market economy, on the basis of capitalist economies with acquisitive aims. Therefore, only the West knows the capitalist form of organization of labor of a purely voluntary nature, from the formal point of view, as the typical and main form of satisfying the needs of broad masses of men, with expropriation of the workers, of the means of production, and with appropriation of enterprises on the part of shareholders. Only the West knows public credit in the form of bonds and financing as the object of rational enterprises, stock exchange trading of commodities and stocks, the "money market" and the "capital market," monopolistic groups as a form of rational organization for acquisitive purposes, of the production of goods on an entrepreneurial basis—and not only that of the sale of goods."[9]

This reprise, this kind of refrain, *"Nur der Okzident . . . ,"* whose exuberance is scarcely and with difficulty kept in check by the analytical seriousness of Weber's scientific prose, can only recall to mind the dithyrambic tone of the pages in Marx and Engels's *Manifesto* in which the bourgeoisie is greeted as a revolutionary force that has swept away traditional uses and customs, freeing mankind from the idiocy of rural life and unifying the planet economically, i.e., practically, penetrating its life with a deep rational need. What for Marx and Engels was, however, the premise for a revolutionary choice, runs in Weber the risk of remaining the expression of an unconscious "filial" emotional attachment.

6. The Utilitarian Mentality

Why, however, is it that only in the West that the rationalization of life has been able to take off and involve the center of economic production, *not* limiting itself to the intellectual sphere—as occurred in other civilizations: mandarins in China, sages in India—but on the contrary also directly influencing the daily round of life? Why only in the West did science not limit itself to being pure speculation, the prerogative of a small, hierocratic elite, but instead, from the beginning of the modern era, became a rational scientific technique, that was applied to the production of goods—thus thereby deeply changing the methods of production and in due course, the modes of life of huge masses of workers?

Weber believed that rationalization of the productive cycle and the application of science to the processes of production would not have been possible without the crucial mediation of a new vision of life and the world, of a previously unheard-of self-image of the human being and, consequently, a new conception of one's own position in the world, one's duties as regards oneself and as regards one's peers. This new vision is found by Weber in the phenomenon, which is typical of Western Europe, of the Protestant ethic, especially in its Calvinist version and in certain other specific Protestant sects. As we have already repeatedly pointed out, however, Weber was not concerned with establishing the philological precision of particular theological texts, but rather to determine how the Protestant ethic was lived and what results it might have in the sphere of economic activity and on practical life in general. It is not surprising that in Benjamin Franklin and in the "utilitarian mentality" that Franklin symbolically represents, Weber should find his "model" or "ideal type" of the new rational man concerned with fitting his desired ends to the means at his disposal: a good administrator of his resources, the judge of his own autonomy, destined to join together wisdom and prosperity, and to enjoy a happy working life, respected by all.

How on the ethical level or that of deeper legitimation can one, however, justify this utilitarian mentality, which while it builds up wealth, has no intention of then enjoying it, as the princes of the Renaissance and the robber barons of the modern age did, but on the contrary tends to reinvest these riches in productive investments, in medium and long-term concerns—that is, concerns which are not speculative—contenting itself with a frugal, simple life spent entirely in the home and workplace? It is the Protestant ethic which justifies and legitimates this utilitarian mentality, with all the attitudes which are its practical corollaries, and it is this religiously justified mentality which sees us witnessing an extraordinary heterogenesis regarding ends. One begins with saving and reinvesting in order to become prosperous and respected in the community, and thus through one's worldly state finds a tangible sign of God's favor and of one's predestination to eternal salvation. One continues to set in motion industrial and commercial enterprises, to work methodically so as to sanctify one's life, and discharge one's duties according to one's *Beruf*—that is to say, profession and vocation taken together. One does not indulge oneself—one does not go to night clubs; one never splurges nor celebrates—not even artistically speaking—but one is plain-living and assiduous in one's work. Thus, one tends to guarantee the salvation of one's soul and ends up by creating the largest of Swiss bank accounts and enterprises with gigantic business profits.

In selecting Franklin as his "ideal type"—that is, to serve as exemplar of the average representative of the new utilitarian mentality—it is doubtful whether Weber made a wise choice. Franklin in character was not at all an average capitalist; he was versatile like Ulysses, a businessman, self-educated, a diplomat, a scientist. He was one of the Founding Fathers and at the same time the inventor of the lightning-rod. His *Autobiography* is in fact more a continuous pleasure for anyone who has not lost —together with a liking for good writing—the somewhat picaresque taste for *tranches de vie* served fresh, *au naturel,* without too many alterations. The texts that Weber greedily quotes are those of the maxims. These seem to him to be pearls which in themselves say more about the "spirit of capitalism" than whole texts: "Remember that time is money. . . . Remember that credit is money. If someone leaves me with his money on account, he gives me its interest, or as much as I in that time can take of it. This increases to a considerable sum if a man has much and good credit and makes good use of it. Remember that money is, by its nature, fertile and productive. Money can produce money, and its fruits can also produce it, and so on. Five shillings, invested, become six, and invested again, seven shillings and three pence, and so forth, until they become a hundred pounds. The more money available, the more one produces in investing it, so thus the amount available becomes increasingly higher. Whoever kills a sow kills all her dependents up to the thousandth piglet. Whoever throws away a crown, *kills* everything which one might have been able to produce with it: [emphasis and exclamation point are Weber's]. Whole series of pounds. Remember that, as the proverb says, he who pays duly on the promised date can at any time borrow all the money his friends have no need of. This is of great use. Together with diligence and sobriety, nothing helps a young person to go ahead in the world so much as punctuality and exactness in all his affairs. Therefore, never hold on to money loaned for one hour more than what you have promised, lest your friend's resentment for the delay close up his wallet for ever. . . ."

This is a fine synthesis of philistinism and a bowing down to the social control of the community. What can lead us to react in these terms is the undoubted fact that whenever Franklin invokes honesty, he does not do so only and exclusively because honesty is a value in itself (the abstract idea leaves him wholly indifferent), but because honesty is useful and allows one to do good business, to make money. It kills two birds with one stone: the conscience is in order, and the wallet is full. Weber is right, however, when he points out that Franklin wants to earn not what he needs, but rather "as much as he can," and that this sporting spirit, as it were, applied to business, is the nucleus of an exclusively Western European phenomenon: "a capitalism existed in China, in India, in Babylon, in antiquity and in the Middle Ages; but . . . it lacked that special ethos."[10]

These interconnections are interesting, but they need to be further illustrated, and they need to be demonstrated not only in regard to non-Christian and extra-European civilizations. This would be basically tiring and would require a great deal of effort given the enormous amount of material and information to be gathered and organized, but it is a task that is still relatively simple. These interconnections have to be demonstrated within Western Europe.

7. Why Capitalism Only in the West

Let us, then, imagine a Weber who confronts the map of Europe and asks himself: why did capitalism, with its antitraditional rationalism, its individualism, and its strictly impersonal bureaucratic administration and the prevalence of finance capital committed to industrial enterprises (property) over income from land, develop above all in the countries of Northern Europe rather than in those of Mediterranean Europe? Furthermore, how was it that in the countries of Northern Europe themselves, and above all in the northern regions of those countries, that capitalism developed with its technical commitments and professional schools, whereas it was in a minority situation in the southern regions of those same countries? Here, Weber acts like a classical sociologist. He does not pose a small specialized problem: (for example, what is the most decisive single determinant variable as regards the morale of the workers of department Z in factory XY?). He asks a question at the macrosociological level regarding a question from which there depends both the "spirit" and also the destiny, the future, of a whole historical epoch. Weber's attitude recalls that of his great contemporary Emile Durkheim, also standing before the map of Europe with a statistical series of suicides at hand, asking himself how it was that the rate of suicides rose in the Northern European countries and fell precipitously, almost to the point of zero, in the Southern European ones. Durkheim thought he had found a meaningful correlation between suicide and the level and type of social cohesion, and found also that cohesion was aided by a religion, like Roman Catholicism, familial, fairly traditional, with confessors who practiced psychotherapy by ear, but also without remuneration, interceding with the Lord God by means of the Virgin Mary and a legion of saints variously specialized in facing the travails of life. Weber's type of response is perhaps more complex. His statistics are less up-to-date, and in any case are harder to interpret, but basically the response is analogous. For Weber, too, the spread of the "spirit" of capitalism had rooted itself, almost like a mass phenomenon, among the Protestants; whereas among Catholics it was either in difficulty or had, in fact, died out. What did this imply? Possibly that the Protestants were more "worldly," more "inhabitants of this world" than Catholics?

Certainly, things are not like this. For with the Reformation, it was not so much the spirit of religion that was weakened. On the contrary, the religious spirit was actually reinforced; the traditional and especially Roman Catholic laxity was severely criticized: "Not an excess, but a defect of religious domination over life, was what the reformers who arose in thethen economically most developed countries found worth attacking."[11] One might think that the Roman Catholics, being a minority, started from positions of relative disadvantage in regard to economic activity and success in business. The whole history of modern industrial economic development, however, demonstrates that it is precisely the work of minorities that generally are more ready to break with routine, to lend themselves to innovations, and thus psychologically tend more to try new directions.[12] Weber cites other facts that seem to him important regarding this question, such as the type of school in which Catholics and Protestants respecitvely enroll their children (humanistic, traditional schools for Catholics, and technical ones for the Protestants), and already at the outset the formulation of his thesis emerges clearly: capitalism spread in particular among Protestants for the simple reason that among them it found the moral and ethical requirements, quite apart from the economic ones, that were suitable to its growth: a religiously regulated life favored the strict professionalization of activities, including economic ones; religious methodism, which is indeed distanced from the world, has meant—and in reality means, without its protagonists' consciously proposing it—an economic and methodically entrepreneurial activity, and thence accumulation of capital, the conquest of markets, and unprecedented industrial expansion. "Still more apparent is the connection, which almost has no need to be recalled, between a religious regulation of life and an intense development of business sense in a great number of those sects whose distance from the world has become proverbial, hand in hand with their wealth. . . ."[13]

The phenomenon which at this point in Weber's argument must be borne in mind is that the concept of "social ethic" on which capitalism is based is not "born in the territory of capitalism"; it comes from other, more remote sources, and it is this concept that in fact must be taken into account in all its ramifications. It is a concept that has religious origins. It is linked to the rules of life that transcend the pure impulsion toward gain. Sociologists rationalize it and make it a simple symptom through which the believer can have the certainty of salvation—that is the certainty of being predestined to gain salvation. Capitalism, for its operations, requires a conception of work as a daily duty for everyone, a duty that extends beyond one's own egotistical needs, a duty that finds in it no place for a hedonistic conception of life. For this reason, the conception of labor that capitalism requires demands an ethical foundation. In Weber's view, however, the only ethic capable of coherently lending such a support or foundation is the Protestant ethic. The alternative lies in believing that one is pushed toward the duty of methodical labor only by "practical rationalism," or "that type of conduct of life which consciously places the world only in relation to the material interests of the single ego, and makes its judgments from this point of view";[14] the latter is a style of life which, according to Weber, is today still the typical characteristic of the people of "free will," the French and the Italians. This alternative might have recourse to at least two arguments: (1) we are not, in fact, conscious today when we go to factory or office of obeying imperatives of a religious kind; but Weber maintains that the contemporary capitalist order is an "enormous cosmos" into which the individual is thrust at birth. It is given to the individual, at least insofar as the person is an individual, as an environment not in practice changeable, not noting that throughout the whole process of primary socialization from birth to six or seven years, a quantity of values and behavior are directly internalized in the child, from first bowel and then bladder control to the ideas of what is good and what is bad; (2) the egocentric hedonism, whilst it can partly explain the drive to maximize one's own material advantages, is not capable of taking into account the basic and essential characteristic of the "spirit of capitalism"—that is, the attitude toward one's own professional vocation as toward a duty whose discharge leaves aside both psychological and financial rewards.

8. The Concept of *Beruf*

We have arrived at the concept of *Beruf*.[15] The religious person can be certain of being in a state of grace and of achieving eternal salvation in two cases: insofar as one feels oneself a recipient, or according to circumstances, insofar as one feels oneself an instrument of Divine Power. In the first case, the religious life is inclined toward the mystique of feeling and tends to be passive, far from the world and its works. In the second case, the religious life tends to be active and presents itself with vigor in order to attain spiritual perfection in this world. Luther mainly approaches the first type, while Calvin belongs to the second. However, Calvin's God, according to his followers, was not content merely with occasional good works. He demanded sanctity of works *elevated into a system*. And here enters the concept of *Beruf*, with its double meaning of "profession," and of "calling," "vocation" in the religious sense. There is no doubt that this meaning of profession, typical of Calvinist Puritans, seems to foreshadow and generally fit the behavior and attitudes of the hyperactive, tireless "demiurgic" "captain of industry," as Schumpeter was later to say—the captain of industry on whom, and on whose innovative hyperactivity would depend the breaking of stagnation and the start of economic development on a vast scale. It is not difficult to grasp in this frenetic activity—which seems to have the accumulation of wealth as its explicit end, but which in reality develops with an intemperance and a taste for activity that places it as an end in itself—the reflection of a deep existential anguish with religious foundations, if not with the direct consequence of the psychological insecurity felt by the individual follower of Calvin as a result of the fact that he can never tell for certain that he is among the elect, and finds himself alone, without the mediation of any church, faced not with the loving God of the New Testament, but rather with the terrible, inscrutable judge who for all eternity has decided who will be saved and who will be damned—the irascible, jealous, and unpredictable God of Israel.

It is, however, also easy to note that the emphasis with which Weber stresses the Calvinist doctrine of grace and predestination is based on a single Calvinist document, not one of the most important ones, whose understanding becomes at least problematic outside its general context:

that is, the *Confession of Westminster* of 1647. Second, and this is a fact which weakens the whole brilliant Weberian scheme, between this document and the particular version of Calvinism that corresponds to it, on the one hand, and the phenomena of the "spirit of capitalism," with the Protestants leading and the Catholics in the rear—both in Europe and in the Grand Duchy of Baden—on the other hand, there is a gap of two centuries, which no sociological subtlety can manage to bridge. Having said this, one cannot deny Weber's acuteness in dealing with the figure and behavior of the virtuous man, according to Calvinist rules, and the effects which these rules have on his daily behavior and attitude regarding the economic sphere. There is no doubt that Weber manages by contrasting Calvin to Luther, selecting certain elements in Calvin's complex doctrine, and emphasizing them, to give us some plausible, explanatory guides which can come to terms with the apparent absurdity of the behavior of individuals who go on working tirelessly day after day to accumulate wealth, even after this accumulation has taken place—with supreme indifference towards it, without relaxation, without enjoying it in any way, as though tied by an obscure curse or committed to a mysterious bet. They work tirelessly because their spiritual perfection, rather than lying in the monastery, is their calling to fulfill it in the world: not through Franciscan contemplation or poverty but in the tumult of an active life whose financial "capitalist" fruits are not meant for the enjoyment of the individual who has produced them, but have the function of demonstrating—if only in a never totally certain and absolute way—that he is regarded by Calvin's terrible God with benevolence, and that perhaps he is included in the small number of those predestined to salvation. No one can know with certainty if he is to be saved or damned. All that one can know for certain is this: That part of humanity will be saved and that another part will be damned.

Weber manages here, leaving aside the question of historical exactitude, to give us the existential dimension of the drama of the Puritan with the power of images that presupposes an abnormal interpretative ability, so as to make the age relive, in its historical situation, the psychological position of its protagonists; and indeed show itself as a transposed reflection of a basic autobiographical experience. "In spiritual care, which for men at the time of the Reformation was most important, being that of eternal health, man was sent forth to follow in solitude his path towards a destiny fixed from eternity onwards. No one could help him."[16] Naturally, the work of mediation of the church was eliminated. The sacraments were liquidated. Even in the burial of their loved ones, the genuine Puritans rejected all trace of ceremony, songs, and music; no magical sacramental element was tolerated. Here Weber had a characteristic brainwave, even though, like every brainwave, it was then difficult to give a precise empirical demonstration for it: "That great historico-religious process of the elimination of the magical element in the world, which began with the ancient Judaic prophesyings, and which with Greek scientific thought rejected all magical means in the search for health, considering them as a criminal superstition, found its conclusion here."[17]

In terms of social organization—which is Weber's concern—this, inasmuch as it was concerned with Catholicism but also Lutheranism, caused a substantial change in attitude as regards that fundamental concept of Christianity, which is "love of one's neighbor." This was a tricky passage. This was the moment in which transition from the religious attitude to the social behavior of the individual in the broadest sense took place, whether as an economic agent in the true sense or as a member of global society. In fact, for the Calvinist as love of one's neighbor should serve only the glory of God and not other human beings, it can and must manifest itself first in the fulfillment of the professional duties imposed by the laws of nature—that is by the laws of nature that are the works of God—and thus take on the objective and impersonal character of a service rendered to the *rational ordering* of the society in which we live. Behind the third edition of Calvin's *Institutio,* in which the doctrine of the *"decretum horribile"* of predestination through grace had its full elaboration, behind the very "spirit of capitalism" which Weber has in mind—and which in his view was created by that doctrine and which still has as its protagonist the individual capitalist, both proprietor and entrepreneur, bound to maximize profits and production to the greater glory of God—there is sketched out the shadow of the great father of "the scientific organization of labour," the Philadelphia engineer in whom Calvinistic pessimism and rationalizing technocratic mentality were mixed in equal parts: Frederick Winslow Taylor.

The fear of being condemned without hope of appeal for all eternity must have been very strong in these Calvinists—future unconscious capitalists. The effects of this fear, however, according to Weber—in Bunyan and in Alfonso de' Liguori, for example—were very different, even radically antithetical. The same fear, that which pushed them toward the deepest humiliation of themselves spurred the former to a systematic, unyielding struggle with life: to change the environment, to organize society rationally. Where does this radical difference come from? Weber believed that he had discovered its origin in the interpretation furnished by Calvinism to the warning of the apostle to consolidate one's own *vocatio* by winning in the struggle—that is, in everyday professional work—the subjective certainty of one's own election and justification. Weber concluded: "The fact that worldly professional work was regarded as valid for this end, that it should be considered. . . . as the means suitable for reacting against religious fears, finds . . . its motivation in deepelements of the religious sensibility cultivated by the reformed church, which later came clearly into the light with their difference with Lutheranism in the doctrine of justification through faith."[18]

9. Critical Questions: Was the Reformation or, indeed, the Counterreformation essential?

Now, for more than fifty years, Weber's thesis on the connection between Protestantism and capitalism has been exposed to an almost uninterrupted fusilade.[19] The thesis still stands. Why? I think one must recognize that the thesis resists because it is formulated in such a way that, if it cannot be conclusively demonstrated as true, neither can it be demolished as false and irrelevant. S. N. Eisenstadt, has, however, diligently gathered a compendium of critiques of Weber primarily favoring relatively recent ones (for contemporaries, Weber's own footnotes in the later editions of his work are sufficient); furthermore, those critics who do not restrict themselves to the famous *The Protestant Ethic and the Spirit of Capitalism,* but rather deal with the examination of Weber's analyses of non-Christian and extra-European religions. Thus, there are citations of Julius Guttman (1925), who finds the break traced by Weber between prophetic and Rabbinical Judaism untenable; J. Katz (1961) observes that in ancient Judaism, religious activities are never sanctioned as the central dimension of human effort. In regard to China and Confucianism, O. Van der Sprenkel (1964) and C. K. Yang (1964) find Weber's analysis even today essentially adequate, while Milton Singer (1961), whose concern is India, mounts against Weber a series of stinging criticisms; namely, that in his study of Hinduism and of Asian religions he simply was not aware of—or had consciously failed to keep in mind—basic elements of Asian religions, such as a component of intramundane asceticism: the economic rationality of merchants, artisans and peasants; a theologically coherent system of impersonal determinism in Vedanta and in Buddhism, with direct consequences for lay ethics, the development of a "rational empirical" science; religious individualism and personal monotheism. Clifford Geertz makes a basic criticism (1956, 1960, 1963) of the one-sidedness and exaggeration of Weber in regard to non-Christian religions, especially those with which Geertz is conversant—that is, those of Java. But even in Geertz's work, one can still see a Weberian starting point. For Japan, Robert Bellah (*Tokugawa Religion;* 1957) finds in the general ethos of the samurai as upheld by the Singaku sect with a combination of Shintoism and Confucianism, the equivalent of the Protestant ethic which became an important factor in the development in a modern direction of Japanese socioeconomic life.

It is, however, in the work of Herbert Luthy that we find a series of critical observations that seem directly to controvert Weber's main argument—that is, the connection between the Protestant Reformation and the development of the spirit of capitalism in Western Europe.[20] The beginning of Luthy's criticism is, first of all, quite like the habitual one made by historians. It is like reading Cantimori or Sestan. For example: "One can repeat with Landshut, that essentially Max Weber's sociology is the attempt to make an analysis of the social formation of the modern era in Europe: a specific, historically determinate social formation . . . but Weber did not stay faithful (as regards conclusions) to the essence, to the basic "intention" of the problem he posed, and strayed away from the critical, historically determinate enquiry into the abstractions of formal sociology. . . ."[21] Luthy's critique, however, if we examine it attentively, becomes more informed, is not limited to repeating the tired prejudice against the formalism of sociology, and gets to the heart of the matter. Luthy begins by saying that it is at least risky to make a great historical event depend on a "single cause," be it spiritual or material. Further, he argues that the schism provoked within Western civilization by the Protestant Reformation did not have the same dramatic character, and did not shake the basic unity of that civilization as, instead, happened with the schism between Rome and Byzantium. After these prudent opening remarks, however, Lüthy raises a doubt about what may be considered the heart of Weber's analysis—that is, the union of the principle of liberty and responsibility of individuals with the principle of rationality. That this union might be the result of Calvinistic Puritanism, and that this product can then be reduced to its manifestation, however obvious, as the "spirit of capitalism," seemed to Lüthy to be wholly unfounded opinions connected to supporting evidence which was either dubious or clearly untenable.

Weber's "proofs" were systematically examined, and from this examination they emerged somewhat shakily. The *Westminster Confession* of 1647, as we noted above, must be resituated somewhat drastically. Connected to its context, it seems more like the expression of a momentary, passing disquiet of the great legislator, statesman, and reformer of Geneva ("more than a dogma, Calvin's predestination is a confession of ignorance and frightened disorientation," p. 12).

Benjamin Franklin's *Maxims*, so sage and amusing in their utilitarian perversion of the imperatives of honesty, are certainly a fine listing of "bourgeois virtues." A century earlier, Jacques Savary had achieved international fame with his operetta, *The Perfect Tradesman*—a pity that Savary was a Catholic. Not only this; but the anguish of the Calvinist's lonely soul, which found in methodical, tireless labor the therapy for his religious terrors, and Franklin's disenchanted, utilitarian morality are not contemporary phenomena. There is, indeed, more than a century between them. How does one best bridge this logical and chronological void?

There is more to consider. In regard to the moral and economic situation of Western European civilization at the time, the Reformation might well be judged a regressive movement. This is the basic premise of the reevaluation proposed by Luthy. Italy and Spain were ready for the genuine capitalist takeoff, not only and not so much with a new ethic of labor, but with all the new attitudes of a civlization ever more scientific and quantative, with the cult of material precision instead of qualitative appreciation, the heir of the great impulse of the Renaissance as illustrated by, among others, John U. Nef.[22] If one were to stage a meeting between characters like the Medici, the Fuggers, Erasmus, Copernicus, Christopher Columbus, on the one hand, and Luther and the other reformers on the other, it is clear that "the least contemporary, the fullest of medieval traditions, was certainly the mind of Luther." Only when one switches one's attention to the reformers of Zurich and Geneva, does a certain affinity between the Reformation and the capitalist spirit appear, for the good—not religious—reason, however, that here we are dealing with men at grips with the concrete practical problems of the economic and social organization of free, commercial cities, for whom freedom from the dead hand of the past is a matter of survival. According to Luthy, there is a very close connection between ethics and work in the Benedictine maxim, "Ora et Labora," as in all Reformation texts. Luthy concludes that "rather than attributing the creation of a new economic spirit to the Reformation, there are excellent reasons for maintaining that by way of the Reformation, the spirit of the medieval urban republics was perpetuated." What prevented this spirit from perpetuating itself and developing itself in the Roman Catholic countries—Italy and Spain, above all—which were at the time the most advanced materially and culturally of the nations of Europe, was the process of stagnation and strangulation operated by the Counter-Reformation. The interpretative point of view, has, thus, to be reconsidered, and must be profoundly changed. It is not the Reformation which generates a new spirit, but rather the Counter-Reformation which retarded the development of the whole of the West for at least two centuries, and particularly suffocated the seeds and embryonic creations of free and modern institutions which already existed in the Catholic countries. One cannot say that Weber's thesis emerges from this critical examination wholly destroyed; yet it is difficult to deny that the brilliant elegance of his comments (from the doctrine of predestination through grace to the individualization of responsibility, from the need of tangible signs of salvation to systematic labor and reinvestment of capital, from the accumulation of capital to the rational calculation of economic expansion and from this ultimately to capitalism on a continual and broader scale) must be harshly and irrevocably compromised.

10. Toward a World of "Functionaries"?

The criticisms of H. Luthy, which are in part far from new, have the merit of punishing the vainglory of sociology, which tends to extrapolate, from a fairly shaky empirical base, generalizations of a scope so broad as to embrace globally whole civilizations and historical periods. Not all

Lüthy's observations, however, especially not those concerning the use Weber makes of the statistics of Martin Offenbacher and the usual importance given to the accuracy of his reading of theological texts—an accuracy reduced to a purely philological exactness in which Weber was neither interested nor bound—are acceptable. What seems to me to be important to keep in mind in these observations, and what in my view can be applied also to many contemporary studies of the so-called crisis of the sacred, is the necessity of a logico-linguistic definition of the terminology used, and of a global vision of the problems, or a vision able to guarantee the analysis of specific situations without at the same time islating them from the broadest context.

Both these necessities cannot be denied to have been present in Weber's consciousness, even if not always with satisfying results. It may well be that he favored, beyond available proof, the weight and function of the movement of the Reformation in regard to the creation and diffusion— up to the point of its becoming a mass ethic—of the spirit of capitalism. No one, however, can hold reasonable doubts regarding the tendency, which is characteristic of Weber, of reading and interpreting every phenomenon of the wider framework of situations and of movement of the whole of society.

Weber's attitude toward the rationalization of life is ambiguous. On the one hand, he hails it as a step of extreme importance in the process of emancipating humanity on the path of free conscious choices on the part of individuals. There is no concession in Weber to the easy feelings of universal benevolence and permissiveness that lie at the basis of the modern welfare state. Every inclination toward hedonism left him indifferent, and in some cases had the power to make him furious. Perhaps he felt instinctively that happiness is in itself vulgar, as is enjoyment: that it is not for happiness and by making things easy that one must struggle, but rather for the freedom to determine one's own life, and hence the dignity of man. In him there was a deep vein of stoicism, which was not by chance connected with Calvinist pessimism, active without hope and without expecting rewards, and that recalls Gramsci's formula of "pessimism of the intelligence and optimism of the will." In this sense, Weber was a true individualist and a true liberal. He had faith in the rationality of individual judgment: he had in mind no alternative to liberal civilization, on the institutional, political level as well as on the economic one, which would not of necessity be a disastrous fall into social chaos dominated by undisciplined masses, incapable of any project. He did not believe that he could submit to any power or authority which was not the result of rational meditation, the result of a calculation that started from the inner tribunal of his own consciousness. Yet, in another sense, with genuine, deep anguish, he was aware of the repercussions of the antitraditionalist movement, which aimed at rationalizing life in respect to the whole of political and social organization, and the very psychic structure of mankind. Did he perhaps sense in rational calculation, behind the precision and the planning ability he hymned, a radical impoverishment, one without salvation? This noble German professor—so much attached to his mother and so sensitive that, in his "crazed and wholly desperate" Leopardian study he had had intermittent recourse of escape by way of terrifying depressions—possibly foresaw the proletarianization of the spirit which, at the end of the First World War, was being prepared and diffused like a leprosy in Europe, in the United States, and throughout the world. Perhaps he understood, or guessed, that behind the social anxiety and propagandist rhetoric of cheap happiness and "free time," there was, rather, the outline of a avoid, and the unsurmountable calm sadness of a society in which, instead of men, there were only functionaries. Once the function has been exhausted, what else can one expect? Once the function has ended, the man/functionary is, literally, defunct.

CHAPTER THREE

THE PROBLEM OF POWER

1. Why Men Obey

Certainly in Max Weber's personality, obscurities, tensions, and ambiguities, both logical and existential, were not lacking. None, however, rivaled the depth of its impact on his life and thought and the anguish it provoked in him as the contradiction entailed in harboring a very strong political vocation, a real drive for action and power, on the one hand, and on the other, the simultaneous need to see clearly and understand in all its implications a given situation before reaching a decision. For Weber, this ambivalence remained an open wound. He managed to be a part-time politician, a politician *manqué*—that is, a politician declining into the role of consultant—and an intellectual who was never resigned to being only a professor and writer of articles, a scholar with a real longing for action.

Among the problems he was involved with, the problem of power in all its important facets does, in fact, stand out. This is an economic problem, linked to stratum and class situations; it is a social problem with the important accompaniments of prestige and deference; it also is a political problem with questions of the state, its structure and government, which express its legitimate power—that is, authority based on consensus— the fullness of *imperium*. In the rich list of themes covered by Weber, the discussion of power in its widest meaning occupies a central position. What is striking is that Weber does not restrict himself to looking at the phenomenon of power from a single point of view. Sociological tradition gave him famous precedents in this regard. For political scientists, power was the problem of the state, of order, and the "social contract"; for sociologists, the tradition had a different emphasis if not nature: this was the problem of consensus and social integration.

Furthermore, in the study of power, the social sciences followed two divergent paths that ultimately tended to become self-contradictory. They considered power as a given in the objective structure of society, a determinate place in the social pyramid; or else power was seen as an interpersonal relation, one between two or more individuals, something fluid, not perfectly ascribable to any position and fixed social function within the productive and distributive cycle of goods. In this context, the most recent sociological and politological tradition confronted in a highly polemical and methodologically hostile manner the traditional Marxist position, which stated that it was absolutely impossible to pose correctly the problem of power except within the struggle of economic interests and in the framework of the dynamics of class struggle.

Even if Marx never explicitly defined the concept of class, or better, even if his ideas on this characteristically varied according to the particular viewpoints from which he was starting (the dualistic vision of the two enemy camps in the *Communist Manifesto* or the much more coordinated and variegated position in his political pamphlets, such as *The Civil War in France* and *The Eighteenth Brumaire of Louis Bonaparte*), it was clear that the class that was dominant in the economic sphere, the bourgeoisie, which held the right of property and the means of production, and was the buyer on the formally free market of proletarian labor power, was also the class in power *par excellence,* and that thus economic and political power coincided. This meant also that state power, and its expression, government, far from representing the people—and still less popular sovereignty—were, notwithstanding the more or less constitutional rites and the extension of the suffrage to the point of being practically universal, nothing more than "the executive committee of the bourgeoisie," its mystifying mask, a legal fiction, a simple screen which, in the name of "public interest," defended and perpetuated the privileges of those who economically already found themselves in a social position of relative advantage.

This conception of power, typically objective and economistic, is a conception of power as zero-sum, which implied and implies dichotomous image of society. Global society here appears as a reality split into two sectors which can neither interchange nor communicate except on the basis of class struggle. There are no margins or no-man's lands. There are those who are up and those who are down, the "superiors" and the "inferiors." Power is monolithic and obeys an iron, systematic logic of development, insensitive or inaccessible to the personal feelings of individuals, which are—by definition—considered irrelevant. Under today's conditions, the burden which rests on those who believe this conception to be plausible and correct lies in the empirical demonstration of the coincidence between political and economic power; that is, the demonstration of the methods and techniques with which the economically dominant class reduces into conditions of subordination and its own service the political class, which is formally elected by the people and representative of the interests of the nation.

Conflicting with this conception is that view of power which hinges on and exalts the psychological elements of the phenomenon. Power is no longer seen here as an objective situation of economic domination. Even the definition of formal prerogatives in a legal sense collapses under skeptical inquiry. Indeed, one tends to emphasize before and against the prerogatives of formally defined powers the importance—official but often, one may say, determining—of "informal power"; that is, of relations of influence, persuasion, prestige, suggestion, authoritativeness, which are not defined or indeed definable in a formal sense, and uncodifiable. These relations of informal power must be decisive, must be "those that count." It is in this way—bearing in mind that informal powers are, by way of being psychological and sociopsychological instruments of analysis—open to measurement and fairly close analytical distinction—that the conception of power, from being an objectively definable situation in that it is tied to the world of economic interests, tends to merge into the network of polydimensional psychological relationships which build up between people independently of class membership and objective involvement in the cycle of production and distribution of goods.

2. The Problematic Nature of Power

One of Weber's great merits is that of being clearly removed from this false dilemma, recognizing in the phenomenon of power the relationship between people, between the governors and the governed, between "top" and "bottom," while recognizing at the same time that this relationship does not take place in a vacuum, that it develops within defined economic systems and political structures, and that the psychological dilution of its terms, although seeming to facilitate scientific research, in reality completely drained it of meaning.[1] With exceptional modernity, Weber escaped both the mechanistic and —even worse—naturalistic determination of a definition so concerned with preserving the objectivity of the phenomenon and its characteristics as to freeze it on a metahistorical plane as well as in the psychologistic trap, for which the "hardness" of the phenomenon of power—that is, its institutional and economic significance —and its political weight tend to dissolve in a more or less idyllic way into the flexible, unpredictable sequence of purely interpersonal relationships. Weber defines power, from the strictly sociological point of view, as the possibility of being obeyed. Hence, it is neither an automatic position of dominance nor an undefinable psychological relationship.

The term *possibility (chance)* introduces into the definition of power an element of indeterminacy, a problematic element of extreme importance. I am not blind to the danger of an interpretation of this definition in purely psychological terms. Certainly the term *chance,* which is basic to Weber's definition, does not exclude but necessarily implies, personal capacity. Furthermore, *chance* is still objective *chance*—fortune in the classic sense. There is the idea of personal ability, together with fortune — of a "feminine" fortune *(fortuna),* dominated and forced into one's own projects, in a Machiavellian sense. This, however, is not in a void, not in a simple, interindividual relation. The power with which Weber is concerned is not just personal ability; this would at once be watered down into some psychological category, such as influence, prestige, authoritativeness. It also depends, one might say dialectically, on the context:— that is, on the structural situation and the objective data in which the phenomenon appears on the historical level, the level of real power relations that are socially significant.[2]

3. The Spirit of the Time

The danger of Weber's definition of power lies in its multivalence. It can be squashed into contradictory usages; it leaves open a series of problems which, for Weber, are quickly seen to be unsolved. Is it possible to base the essential legitimacy of power—that is, to transform it into authority—using as a basic criterion of justification and legitimization the majority opinion of an undifferentiated mass?

It is impossible to correctly evaluate and interpret Weber's position in this regard with its great merits, which we have stressed, though also with its unsurmountable limitations, which are undeniable and often damaging, without recalling—however briefly and summarily—the general political and intellectual climate in which Weber lived and worked. Naturally, to reconstruct the cultural outlook and intellectual atmosphere of a period is in itself a difficult undertaking. In the present case, we are dealing with a historical phase which, probably by sinister irony, was given the name of *"la belle epoque,"* extending more or less from 1870 to 1914, as it was precisely during this period that the seeds for the two catastrophic world wars of the first half of this century were sown.

For Weber, there was not just the question of surpassing the limitations of his family background and the special culture related to it, in which he operated during the process of his primary socialization. There was also the question of overcoming the limitations—the prejudices, the commonplaces, one might say that conditioned reflexes of his own time. This period in the first place was dominated by an elitism which could only reinforce that already absorbed from his earliest childhood years. His father was a successful man, a jurist, a councillor, going from the Diet of Berlin to the Prussian Diet and eventually becoming a member of the Reichstag. He knew the rules of the society to which he belonged and knew how to use them. He never made a false step. In the family he was somewhat of a disaster, but in society he never made a gaffe. Weber's mother was sensitive; with origins in the world of the petite bourgeoisie, she had a lot of dignity and little money; she possessed much sense of duty, of position and the vital necessity of distinguishing oneself at the level of values from the *parvenu,* from whom it became increasingly difficult to distinguish oneself on the level of purchasing power. It was with his mother that Weber talked and communicated; he also wrote her letters of high intellectual content. The interlocutor mother found in her son the compenstaion for an unsatisfactory relationship with her husband. There were already uncles and relatives in the academic sphere; a family background of army officers, state bureaucrats and academic intellectuals, professors, teachers. In families of this kind, distance and distinction are occasionally sought for, as we have noted, on the level of personal individual value, through an obsessive insistence on the merits of the individual, in the fetishism of "values," and the selective criterion which establishes the excellence of each person independently of the fact that in everyday life one must live shoulder to shoulder with the plebs, the little people.

This vertical tension, this need for distinction, this enormous "achievement complex," as the psychologist MacLelland would say, is possibly at the root of the nervous exhaustion and recurrent mental disturbances from which Weber suffered and which eventually all too clearly betray the painful sense of an objective status imbalance acutely perceived, the fall of a world of fixed and well-defined differentiations, the unconsciously feared advance of the egalitarianism typical of a mass society then beginning—which was by definition a denial of the standards of individual excellence—the pitiless leveler of all elites, in every field, ready to commodify by lowering all noble values in the name of merely functional needs. Weber's very prose is obsessional; the sentence, so classically arranged in its general, predetermined structure, breaks between his hands, and does not stand up to the shock of the impulsion that comes from within; it is unable to exorcise its writer's anguish.

Weber was an elitist, a logical one, to the furthest degree. His main concern from the political point of view was the preparation of a directing elite, German-centered and aristocratic. It is in this sense that elsewhere I have described Weber as "Bismarck's Orphan," despite the fact that Prussia, Bismarck, and traditional precapitalist, agrarian Prussian Junkerdom, which was almost archaic, were his habitual targets. One often attacks ferociously what one loves. Weber criticized Prussia with tart bitterness, but he adored and wanted to preserve for the whole of Germany, the authentic virtues of Prussianism: faithfulness to duty, resolute toughness in action, a seriousness so immovable that it might seem to be stolid, and the Catilinarian rage of decisions which he never tired of contrasting with ornate irresponsible eloquence and Cicero's clever weakness.

He is thus a man who identified himself with a small group of chosen people. If his circle in Munich did not have the exclusive character of that of the poet and aesthete Stefan George, it was nonetheless always a circle of initiates, open only to those who had eyes to see and ears to hear. Like the Thomas Mann character, Hans Castorp, a man of the plain forced to live in the world, he, too, aspired to his "magic mountain." In the world surrounding him, which was rapidly being transformed into a mass industrialized society, he resigned himself to live only to see how long he could resist. Hence derives his stoicism, but also his ambivalence, lack of resolution, and the unravellable knot of his neurosis. There is a basic ambiguity in Weber which seems to me to be the opposite of, but also symmetrical to, Thomas Mann's. They are both representatives of the *haut bourgeois,* although wholly different temperamentally. Mann is serene, Olympian, "a representative more than a martyr . . . stubborn owner of villas," the splendid product of an assured age that is, however, being eroded and undermined, and whose ruin expresses underground presentiments and subtle metaphors. Weber was hard, suffering, and anguished: He was ambiguous, too, if only with a "theorized" ambiguity, able to work on himself in the flesh, an exemplary case of self-surgery. Perhaps, in order to understand and prepare the raw materials needed to reconstruct the mental climate of Weber's period, the essential text is precisely Thomas Mann's *Considerations of an Unpolitical Man.* Here, there spills out that visceral pan-Germanism which lies at the bottom of Weber's complaint that "world politics are no longer made in Berlin."

Then, not admitted but ever-present, with that halo of romanticism of the science that is the true, unique religion of the "free spirits" of the nineteenth century, there is Darwin. The "struggle for existence," is a principle not only valid in the field of the study and life of nature. It is a dogma beyond discussion, which is a granitic support for the stupid cruelties of current morality. If there were no struggle for existence, continual and universal, from the inorganic "kingdom" to the vegetable one, thence to the animal, and ultimately to the human and social realm, how could one guarantee the survival of the most suitable and thus the general "improvement" of the human race? One is not far from quoting the scriptures, "It is necessary that one die for the good of the people. . . ." From here to the acceptance, indeed, to the approval of war, however, the passage is dangerously brief. War is considered a normal affair; it enters into the plans and predictions of normal administration. Nowadays one says with an apprehension that is more or less troubled, "If war comes. . . ." Then, in Mann and Weber's time, one said, "When war comes, . . ." and prognoses were made and bets were laid on who would win it, and who would fight against whom. This, therefore, was war as normal administration, as a martial exercise: war, moreover, as a necessity.

In the *Manifesto* of his movement (1909), the founder of futurism, Filippo Tommaso Marinetti, asserted, "War is the only hygiene of the world . . . ," which was immediately taken up by nationalists, followers of D'Annunzio, and fascists *avant la lettre*. This is the mentality that still today is reflected in the words of those professors, educationalists, sensitive souls who, faced with the excesses of the youth and student protest, let go with a "we need a war. . . ." Faced with the fascistic basis of this pedagogic hope, they respond as some years ago the literary critic George Steiner replied to me, "Virtue does not have the monopoly on truth"; that is to say, that war is the only hygiene for the world is a truth, even if asserted by futurists, fascists, and decadent aesthetes. For nationalists like Weber, war could indeed develop civic and personal virtues that were highly desirable: solidarity, physical and moral courage, a sense of identification with the ends of the community, love of one's country, altruism. War, therefore, not simply as a purifying cesspit of society but as a selective filter and proving ground of the "brave." Here, racial discrimination is grafted on; there are superior races and inferior races, races of naturally victorious "gentlemen" because they are more endowed, mentally and physically "better," and slave races destined to defeat because they are lightweight and mentally and physically retarded. Even within this choice, however, there are groups that are bound to rise and groups that inevitably decline. This is the hard, universal, basically just "law of life." And so, why worry about those who don't manage to keep up? What sense of there in speaking of the "social question"? It is natural that in the world there are rich and poor, just as is natural that alongside the sturdy oak, tall and leafy, there is the humble, fresh fern frond destined sometimes, alas, to be trodden on. However, just as it is natural that in the world there are rich and poor, it is also natural that the poor are hungry. Indeed, basically it is a good thing that the poor are hungry; it has a pedagogic value for all the others; it teaches them to be prudent and frugal, industrious in work and methodical in the conduct of their lives. It is also good, if one looks at things with scientific attention, that the poor end by dying prematurely, because only thus will the better-endowed survive—those most suited to the struggle for existence.

4. The Authority of the Eternal Yesterday

The basic question remains: why did the poor not rebel? Why did Spartacus fail? Why do men obey?

Spartacus failed and men obey, first of all, because men are creatures of habit. Weber outlined in *Economy and Society* the "three pure types of a legitimate domination *(legitime Herrschaft.)*" Human beings basically obey for three reasons: (1) because of the authority of the "eternal yesterday"; (2) because of a feeling for legality; (3) because of what Weber calls charisma, that "specific gift of grace" which can take over a person, granting him extraordinary, more than everyday powers; and by means of this grace he is followed and obeyed. Weber speaks of "pure types," because he is aware that in historical reality none of the three types, which he outlines, is actually manifest with all the characteristics that define it. We are dealing with a "sociological typology." If Weber has really produced it, the basic reason is to be looked for in his conviction that "sociological typology offers to the empirical work on historical research simply the advantage—which, however, should not be underestimated—of being able to determine, in the individual case, what it is in a form of power that has a "charismatic," "charismatic-traditional," "bureaucratic," "of stratum" character, etc., or whether one draws near to these types and works with concepts which are to some extent univocal."[4] And Weber adds immediately afterward, thrusting off any temptation of inerpretation in a purely methodologistic sense, or of confusion between purely logical schemas and actual historical reality, given and concrete: "We are here very far from believing that the whole historical reality lets itself be "imprisoned" in the conceptual scheme being developed."

Traditional power bases its legitimacy on the powers of mastery and on ancient orders ("eternally in existence"). Hence, this is a power not clearly —that is, not formally—established; with objectively codified rights and duties. On the contrary, it is a personal power. The person endowed with the traditional type of power is, however, not a "superior" person, is not invested with power by reason of his personal merits. One obeys traditional power, and the person who is endowed with it, independently of individual qualities, by virtue of the "dignity attributed by tradition." Thus, the traditional chief does not have functionaries in his administrative apparatus but "servants." There are no "members" of the group but "subjects." The key word in this type of power, which points to the normal situation in which it is exercised, is the "loyalty" to him who holds power: "competence," "rational hierarchy," "taking on of power regulated by contract," "specialized preparation," "a stable money salary" — are all characteristics that are either lacking, or at least not required in the practical exercise of traditional power. The principle types of traditional power, in fact, according to Weber, are present when, in the practical exercise of power, the traditional chief does not have at his command a personal administrative apparatus. Then, we have the situations indicated by the terms "gerontocracy," "patriarchy," "patrimonialism."

Weber's analysis is very sophisticated regarding subdivisions of these ramifications of traditional power, but it is particularly alert — as we might logically expect, having seen how the arrival of rationalization and rational calculation in the economic sphere is one of Weber's basic problems — to the relations that are set up between traditional power and economics. In this regard Weber points out that traditional power influences the type of "economic action," in general, by reinforcing the traditional outlook, especially when we are dealing with pure gerontocratic and patriarchal power. Specifically, it has an influence according to the typical mode of financing the power group.

5. Bureaucratic Power

Legal power, with its administrative bureaucratic apparatus, is antithetical to traditional power. Weber deals with this kind of power before the other two — traditional and charismatic — "so as to be able subsequently to compare it with the others." From the point of view, however, of historical development and institutional evolution, as well as logical development, bureaucratic power — or the "power of the general formal rule" — follows traditional power.

In contrast to traditional power and, as we shall see, to charismatic power, bureaucratic power is impersonal. "Superiors" and "subordinates" all obey the impersonal order, and obey as joint members, not as subjects. Furthermore, the members of the group, according to the wielder of bureaucratic power, obey not this person, but impersonal orders, and thus are constrained to obedience only within the limits of their objective, rationally determined, competence, which by these orders is committed to the "superior." The description of bureaucratic power set out by Weber is still rightly famous today, with its starting point or tacit presupposition of studies in the sociology of organization and public administration. The principle of the "hierarchy of offices," of the "rationality of the rule," of the "nonappropriation of the office" by whoever holds it, of "conformity to the acts" of the administration, are described by Weber and discussed with such sharpness that, notwithstanding the notable progress in the administrative sciences, both from the juridical as well as the sociological and psychological point of view, Weber's findings remain a complex of essentially valid proposals. There is no doctrine of the state that can do less as, in any case, there is no rational, formal organization, public or private (a ministry like a clinic, a school, a trade union, or a party), which can be sociologically analyzed either as a formal or informal structure by departing from Weber's contributions in this field.

The critical demands one can make of Weber's construct are well known; with good reason; I have alluded to them elsewhere. One can point out that Weber's conception does not bear in mind the most important fact of our time: the passage from a legalistic bureaucracy of simple guardianship to a dynamic initiating bureaucracy. In the plan of Weber's research, however, pessimism regarding bureaucratic power, supported by well-backed analyses of the Germany in which he lived, was concerned to prepare, *sensim sine sensu,* almost unconsciously, in basic harmony with the premises and individualistic attitude of his methodology and his family traditions and social origin, the resolving moment, the theorization and justification, of the third pure type of legitimate power—the charismatic type.

6. The Charismatic Leader

Charismatic power is always, of necessity, the power of a person, the individual. In this sense, it seems a type of power close to traditional power, which is likewise an eminently personal type of power. In reality, it is traditional power's radical negation. In fact, whereas traditional power has no other basis of legitimation than tradition, charismatic power is based on a denunciation and negation of tradition. In fact, for Weber the emblematic type of charismatic leader is the Jewish prophet who raises himself above the crowd, with no qualification and without any entitlement, powerful only in the mysterious, divine "outburst of grace," which forces him to take a position against everything which makes up routine matters of common administration, the normal manner of doing things and thinking: "It is written . . . But I say unto you. . . ." As a secondary type, Weber sees a kind of charismatic leader in the great political, parliamentary leader, who has the majority in his hand and presses it beyond its small personal interests toward his projects as a statesman which deeply affect the historical level.

It is clear that charismatic power seems equally antithetical to legal bureaucratic power. This latter type of power is suitable for resolving routine questions; it stresses the monotonous rhythm, ever the same, of the institutional rules that watch over the good functioning of the administrative machine. As soon, however, as the community finds itself having to confront an emergency situation, bureaucratic power, faced with a new phenomenon and unforeseen requirements, goes into crisis and confines itself to the defense of the principle of bureaucratic continuity. "Charismatic power is as counterposed to rational power—above all the bureaucratic kind—as to traditional power, and especially to patriarchal and patrimonial power or the power of wealth. Whilst the former two are indeed specific forms of *ordinary* power, (genuinely) charismatic power is really the opposite. Bureaucratic power is specifically rational in the sense that it is bound by rules which are open to be discursively analyzed. Charismatic power is specifically irrational in the sense that it absolutely lacks rules. Traditional power is tied to precedents which took place in the past, and as such it is equally directed on a basis of rules. Charismatic power, on the other hand, inverts the past (within its own context), and it is in this sense specifically revolutionary. . . . It is legitimate only insofar as, and so long as, personal charisma "stands up" in face of the test: this means it finds its recognition from the trusted individual, the disciple and the follower, so long as the leader's charismatic certainty lasts."[5]

Of three pure types of legitimate power, charismatic power is thus the only "revolutionary" power. But here we must be clear. In fact, we are dealing with an essentially elitist revolution worked from above, or a revolution intuited, proclaimed, and ultimately completed by the "great individual," whether he identifies himself with Carlyle's hero, with the "representative man," or the "oversoul" of Emerson, with the prophet of the Jewish tradition or with Nietzsche's "superman." In any case, the charismatic leader is extraneous to the economy; he despises and indeed rejects the economic use of the gift of grace as a source of income. Weber notes in conclusion: "Almost all the prophets were maintained by begging. St. Paul's words, directed against missionary parasitism, 'he who does not work shall not eat," do not naturally signify any approval of 'economics' but only the duty of seeking necessary sustenance "through an accessory trade."[6]

7. The Political Dilemma of Germany

It is too easy to point out the missing links or the types and subtypes overlooked or simply forgotten in Weber's typology. When he spoke of pure types of legitimate power, Weber did not think of them as a systematic methodology inspired by a purely analytical motive. When he spoke of power, he had in front of him — and never forgot for a single moment — the concrete, burning political problem of post-Bismarck Germany. The real reason that all Weber's books are *livres d'occasion* is this: He did not write for writing's sake, nor did he write to make a position for himself in the academic hierarchy — he had the good fortune to find himself provided with that for a good while — nor did he write for fame. He wrote, he researched, he established historic comparisons sufficient to make one dizzy, only because he had before him a specific, circumscribed, highly clear problem. This was the problem of Germany and the form of political power most suitable, capable of guaranteeing a positive, rational future for the Germany that he saw in the insensitive hands of the Emperor William II, whom he considered — though a monarchist by family tradition and personal conviction — a dangerous madman. From this point of view the distance between Weber and modern political scientists, ready to concern themselves with anything so long as they find someone who will pay for it, is incalculable.

The Germany of Weber's time seems triumphal and obtuse at one and the same time. The victory over France at Sedan (1870) had gone to its head. No one took into account that "a great victory is a great danger," especially since more than conquering France on the battlefield was needed if Germany was to take over French culture. The few dissenting voices in the triumphant choir that fed the foreboding pan-Germanism of the tragic adventure of the First World War were isolated, without a public, and in that instant, fell into the void. One thinks of the *Considerazioni inattuali* of Nietzsche: this is the work of a poet and classical philologist, who alone saw further and with greater clarity than all the statesmen and professional political analysts combined.

Although a pan-Germanist and a monarchist, although obsessed by the idea that a great people could not exist without having a great policy unrolled and activated on the world scale, Weber did not fall into the nationalistic ecstasy that seemed to take hold of the large majority of students of political and social problems, and not only extremists like Treitschke. Weber's nationalistic tendency is indisputable. It even inspired at times particular conclusions for his empirical research, and he was well aware of this. To cite a significant episode, in 1893 Weber, the newly named professor of Political Economy at the University of Freiburg, became a member of the Circle of Social Policy *(Verein für Sozialpolitik)*, founded and directed by the "socialists of the chair" (G. Schmoller, A. Wagner, and L. Brentano). Weber had received from the circle the responsibility for carrying out an inquiry regarding the conditions of peasants in East Prussia, on the banks of the river Elbe. In connection with this research, he had read a report to the *Verein* and to the Fourth Evangelico-Social Congress, together with Paul Gohre, which gave rise to a violent reaction on the part of the conservative National Liberals and the Social Democrats, who accused him of "nationalism." The Christian-Social movement then split, producing a progressive wing (Naumann, Schulze-Gavernitz, Göhre, Weber) and a conservative wing, led by Adolph Stocker. No doubt this is a minor footnote on past political maneuvers without a future. What is still of interest today, however, is that the violent reaction was provoked by the conclusion of the report in which Weber accused the nobility and the great Prussian landowners of "national betrayal" because they were "de-Germanizing" Eastern Germany by "importing" foreign workers—Poles—who, above all, were satisfied with lower wages than German workers.

The limits of Weber as a politician are evident. One may perhaps disagree with the interpretation of Weber the politician, provided by W. J. Mommsen,[7] as that of a conscious chauvinist and imperialist forerunner, but it is incontrovertible that Weber remained essentially a nationalist who understood problems of political, institutional, and economic development as a function of national interests.

This passionate nationalist, however, was not shortsighted, nor was he a *tête-bornée* like so many of his colleagues. No professorial ostentation clouded his vision. The victory over France, the great industrial development, the entry of Germany into the rank of the great imperial powers, not only did not lead him toward a self-complacent attitude, but rather filled him with genuine concern. He saw Germany faced with a dilemma without an exit. Either one chose the line of Prussian *Junkertum,* agrarian and regressive, unable rationally to lead the growing power of a great developing country, or one had to decide in favor of an antitraditionalist, modern, functional capitalism, capable of guaranteeing economic expansion and of preparing the ground for "directed" political democracy. To Weber it was clear that the will and strength to open up this second alternative, the only one available which had a minimum of future, was totally lacking. The ruling groups were inept and inadequate. Left to themselves, they would lead the country to ruin. The harshest criticism as regards the ruling class in power—that is, the Junkers with the Liberals, their natural allies when faced with the danger represented by the Social Democrats—did not, however, for Weber imply any indulgence or concession to the latter, or in general to the progressive positions that the opposition represented. Weber was never able to allow himself to accept the Social Democrats, whom he believed to be "politically immature." This is a grave condemnation, with no appeal, as in Weber's language, the phrase means that the Social Democrats were unable to understand the function of violence in the development of historical forces, to understand and take over the logic of power.

8. Democracy Between Bureaucracy and Caesarism

The impasse in Weber's view can be expressed in the following terms. Bureaucratic power is politically irresponsible, but a parliamentary democracy of the Anglo-Saxon type is not practicable in Germany. Therefore, on the horizon we see the ghost of Caesar; that is to say, the shadow of the leader by plebiscite.

In order to understand in its full significance the problem that Weber posed in this respect, one must bear in mind what in his view bureaucracy and bureaucratic control represented. As an authentic individualist, Weber analyzes the pure type of bureaucratic legal power, but he also grasped its repercussions on the economic and social life of Germany in his own time. For him, bureaucratic power was the real leprosy of modern times. The tyranny of this impersonal, repetitive, anonymous, and omnipresent mechanism seemed to him to be the only truly invincible tyranny from which there opened no emergency exits. For classical tyranny there is always the extreme remedy of tyrannicide, but how can one fight this bureaucratic tyrant, faceless or with too many faces? As a practical measure, as an antidote to the power of the bureaucrats, Weber advocated parliamentarism. In Germany, in his view, this remedy cannot function, because the German *Reichstag* is not a true parliament: it is not, in fact, independent of bureaucracy. Worse still, not only is it not independent, but it is literally pervaded by bureaucrats who are elected as deputies without giving up their titles and their ties with the bureaucratic machine. The apathy of the Germans, the foolishness of the crown, the mediocrity of the politicians, among whom one finds no real statesman—nowhere is there any person or institution able to slow down the abuses of the bureaucratic structure that has taken the power of the state into its own hands without assuming any responsibility for it and thereby condemning it to stagnation and lethargy, watched over by the guardianship of these new mandarins.

It is surprising that Weber, so sharp in his diagnosis, does not even try as an experiment or in a simply hypothetical manner, to design an alternative that might hinge—in a new way and without going through tiresome mediations—on the subaltern population which is always, among the various actors in the drama or the comedy of society, directly concerned. Once more the elitist limitation of Weber emerges here, and has its effect. He is simply incapable of understanding a broadly based social democracy. When he is forced to do so, he arrives at a kind of vague populism, with the theorization of the leader by plebiscite, together with the Caesarist leader, a subtype, or more precisely a stepping stone, toward the charismatic leader, who stands above all of these. Weber says: "The political leader arrives at a position of command . . . by winning the loyalty and faith of the masses to his person and his power, by means of demogogic tricks directed precisely towards the masses. In particular circumstances, this means making use of a Caesaristic method in choosing the political leadership."[8]

9. The Problem of Forming a Leadership: Political Parties

It seems almost unbelievable that an analyst of Weber's sharpness would cite parliament and political parties as possible training grounds for the formation of a political leadership worthy of the name. It seems clear that Weber is, in this respect, dazzled by the British example, which in any case is rather idealized. Today his predictions on the evolution of political parties are more important and have basically been borne out. Weber sees with extreme clarity the inevitable need for the bureaucratization and continuous organization—one that is structured and not set up only at election times—of modern mass political parties. Not only this, he further foresees with startling accuracy all the paraparty organizations that the mass party needs in its task of subsidiary organization (youth groups, recreational circles, holiday camps, schools for militants, welfare centers, charities, and so forth). In other words, Weber anticipates the sunset of notable leaders and the arrival of the technicians and party functionaries as firmly ensconced. One no longer lives for one's own politic faith; one lives from it. One feeds from one's own values. Hence derives the professionalization of political men. From this, however, also derives the decline and then the disappearance of the political man as Edmund Burke and Alexis de Tocqueville understood him—a man in the service of the nation, but in the first place a man at peace with his own conscience, capable of individual judgment, not tied to any "party discipline." This perfect consistency remains in Weber as an acute nostalgia, the highest point of a past gone for ever. Closed to the idea of a democracy different from that of the notables, with a broad social base, capable of fleshing-out purely formal legitimacies by connecting the decisions of power to the real needs of the great majority, and, on the other hand, without illusions as to the low *camarilla* of the pseudo-democratic government of his time, Weber sets off down the path of irrationalism by separating the political moment from that of rational lucidity. He even arrives at the point of seeing in political activity a series of decisions based on the blade of pure intuition, on the fragile convergences of interests and the simple management of procedural techniques.

10. Politics as a Diabolic Pact

In Weber, the discussion and judgment of the question of power have undoubtedly matured in such a way as to avoid the pitfalls of methodological formalism and psychologizing dilution. However, Weber, once arriving at the crucial moment of the choice between the world of the notable leader, which he sees as collapsing, and the social enlarging of the very basis of power, does not manage to resolve this impasse. With the instinctive strength of a conditioned reflex, he again takes up the theory of the "great man," and invokes the charismatic leader.[9] Unfortunately, this invocation was not only translated into an analytical or interpretative mistake; it became a political error, and it found—thanks to Weber's attention—a juridical expression in the Weimar Constitution, in the famous Article 48, the *Diktatur Paragraf,* on the basis of which powers were given to the *Reichsprasident* ("President of the Reich")—broader and more compelling powers than those that had traditionally been given to and exercised by the emperor, and which unhappily were to favor the "legal" rise to power of Adolf Hitler. Weber's good intentions are unquestionable. On the political and historical level, however—and it was Weber who so instructed us—good intentions count for little. In Weber's defense, it has been pointed out that, together with Article 48, which expressed his distrust regarding a popular representation that was too "excessive," "fragmented," "incoherent," and which saw in the "paternal hand" of the president, over and above the parties, a possibly necessary moderator, there were also included, on Weber's insistent request and advice, Article 43—which provided for the removal of the head of state—and Article 44—which sanctioned the power of parliamentary enquiry. Even the most stubborn defenders of Weber, however, recognize that "in the light of the political realities we see, retrospectively, that the idea [of Article 48] was an unfortunate mistake."[10] Articles 43 and 44 remained in fact a dead letter. This was not true of Article 48. It was an unfortunate error, and at the same time a tragic irony that a liberal concern for the defense of personal values involuntarily contributed to smoothing the path to Nazism.

CHAPTER FOUR

THE SOCIOLOGY OF UNIVERSAL RELIGIONS

1. Weber and Vulgar Anti-Marxism

Max Weber's comparative studies in the sociology of religion are justly famous and well known even by the nonspecialist. One certainly cannot say that Weber's argument concerning the connection between lived ethics and the forms of economic life has not had recognition. From its first publication in the *Archiv für Sozialwissenschaft und Sozialpolitik* (vols. 20 and 21, 1904-1905), *The Protestant Ethic and the Spirit of Capitalism* quickly became a kind of best seller (even in Italy after 1938, it was known to the average reader in the adequate translation by Pietro Burresi, accompanied by a long, learned even if in some ways misleading — introduction by Ernesto Sestan.)

It was, however, precisely this widespread fame that made the work seem to be born of a suspect origin, or at least to promote a vulgar interpretation of Weber's argument so simplified that it verged on the arbitrary. There is no question but that the exceptional good fortune of Weber's essay *The Protestant Ethic* in the first decade of this century was due in large part to the "upsetting," which many claim to see in it, of the Marxist thesis relating to the genesis and functioning of the capitalist system of industrial production, as well as, in a broader context, of the materialist interpretation of history. For anyone aware of the violent, idealistic, and spiritual reaction which precisely in those years was appearing in Europe against evolutionism and positivism in the first instance, and thereafter, by logical extension, against any coherently materialistic approach to scientific inquiry and against the very idea of science, understood as empirically verified intersubjective knowledge, Weber's good fortune in respect to this work and the reverberation of his position, need no further comment.

These were the years in which there were emerging and imposing themselves on the theoretical level, first Henri Bergson's contribution of "creative evolution," which literally "corrected" Darwinian and Spencerian evolution of the species; of Italy's neoidealism, in the versions of Giovanni Gentile and, especially, Benedetto Croce, who as soon as he had finished the reduction of Marxism to a simple manual of historiographical inquiry—in *Materialismo storico ed economia marxista*—and broken relations with his master, Antonio Labriola, hastened to publish *La Critica*, heralding neo-Kantianism, the approach of the "new historical school" and the ever-clearer contrast between *Kultor* and *Zivilisation* in Germany, which were little by little to prepare and eventually lead to the prevalence of culturalogical explanation of social phenomena and to an ambiguous critique of science in the name of a knowledge neither stipulated nor intersubjective, of a paramystic and religious essence. In Max Scheler and Edmund Husserl's phenomenology, the premise to the tragic "decisionism" of existentialism, and the empty, foolish anguish of irrationalism, in the two symmetrical acceptances of extraworldly mysticism and a vitalism without logical protection.

Simultaneously, on the practical, political level, Marx's revisionism prepared for and justified the accommodations and reformist disavowals of the Second International, while the European power system, with the violent upsurge of nationalism and with the crisis and then the fall of working-class internationalism and international solidarity, foretold the outbreak of the First World War and presented itself as a sinister prelude to the rise of Fascism and Nazism. From the point of view of the individual, intellectual journey with regard to the passage from scientistic positivism to spiritualism, during the years at the turn of the century, and thence the "return to the fold" ' in the bosom of the Roman Catholic Church, the case of Charles Péguy is symbolic. An even more dramatic example, however, though one not free from the tones and essence of a clownish opportunism, occurred a few years later in Italy with the "conversion" of Giovanni Papini, that "played-out/finished" man, who from "cerebral Don Giovannism," approached religious experience, lived as planned irrationality, and a notion of homeland as the single source of real values according to the antiquated national Fascist clichés of the time, backed also by the representatives of the supposedly universal church.

It seems clear that Max Weber, with his category of "the spirit of capitalism," and hence recognition of the importance of non- and extra-economic elements in the explanation of its birth, leaped into that turbulent, noisy current of thought. He did this, however, with a dignity and a firmness of information and a breadth of vision that should be recalled and reasserted. To place and ultimately to drown Weber's voice among those of the nationalist pack, as has been done, ends up by being more than reaching a scientifically untenable conclusion; it is a moral affront. Weber's patriotism had nothing shabby or mean about it. In no way was it comparable to the xenophobia of the village idiot, nor could it legitimately be presented as "the last refuge of the scoundrel." His notion of "the spirit of capitalism" did not, on the other hand, present itself as a one-sided postulate beyond question. It was essentially an heuristic instrument, the formation of an important element, but not the only one, of a great historical-evolutionary hypothesis at the macrosociological level. In reality, Max Weber, in my view, was not interested in polemics; he held that to be contingent, even though all his theoretical work and scholarly effort went to test the Marxist hypothesis itself—by widening, however, its terms—considering it, that is, as an ideal-typical construct, and hence, to a certain extent, arbitrary and unilateral. The popular acceptance of Weber's position in the sense of fashionable anti-Marxism, though responsible for his rapidly established reputation among the public, distorts his seriousness.

Weber's intention was different, and deper, There was, first of all, the need—most pressing to him throughout his life—to come to clear terms with himself regarding the essence of what is "modern," and the meaning, apparently swiftly identifiable but in reality elusive and ambiguous, of rationalism as a theoretical construction and practical rationalization of social life in bureaucratic-organizational terms and in its historical origin. Thus one can say that far from simplistically wanting to overturn and thus throw out the whole of the theoretical and practicopolitical problems posed by Marxism, all his life Weber openly or elusively was conversing with Marx, desperately trying to preserve the autonomy, however, reduced and relative, of the "realm of ideas."

In other words, Weber was perfectly aware of the existence of a debased popularization of Marxism, derived from a hasty mechanistic interpretation of the thought of Marx and Engels. Basically, this was the same interpretation against which Antonio Labriola fought in Italy with exceptional vigor, believing it responsible for hybrid, intellectually irresponsible theoretical constructs—"lorean" in the real sense, as Gramsci was later to say—and on the political level a source of confusion and approximation fatal in its effect on the working class. This philosophically impoverished and dedialecticized form of Marxism, reduced to a dogmatic formula that was little more than a catechism, had already been condemned by Weber in the introduction to *The Protestant Ethic:* "We shall speak later in detail about the conception of ingenuous historical materialism—that certain ideas (those, that is, which make up the *ethos* or spirit of capitalism) become manifest as "reflections" or "superstructures" of economic situations."[2] Just as it is not scholastically legitimate to contrast Weber's argument to Marx's positions, critically understood— that is to say, correctly understood in their dialectic and dynamic sense— so, in my view, it is necessary to recognize that Weber's investigation can correctly be made to take its place in the context of a sociology of the capitalist phenomenon, globally conceived as a group of aspects—economic, political, juridical, cultural, and social—dialectically bound together and ineracting on each other, without being able a priori to postulate that between these aspects there is something of a decisiveness or monocausality, except in a relative sense and in a specific historical context.

It is not by chance that Weber's expansive research begins with a question which concerns the assertion of modern science in the West and the economic and cultural phenomena connected to it: "By what chain of circumstances, here in the West, and only here, have the cultural phenomena been produced which . . . have been found in a strategy of development of *universal* significance and validity?"[3]

It is amazing that Weber, a scholar still only recently and authoritatively reproved by Lukács for having severed the connection between economics and other forms of human activity, should explicitly connect the self-assertion of science in the West to the possibility that it offers practical, lucrative applications and thence leads to the creation of a continuous economic activity through time, generating fair profits and held together and developed on the basis of rational calculation. Rational calculation, that is, in the relationship between costs and returns as well as in the methodical forecasting of future developments: it is thus linked not so much to the occasional exploits of a piratical predatory capitalism, as to the concept and daily practice of *Beruf*, understood in the double sense of religious "vocation" and secular "profession." In this view, earnings do not seem the supreme end, but just the pure and simple external symptom, almost a confirmation, which is not strictly necessary, that individuals and whole human groups are living the "right life" according to the teachings of the Scriptures.

2. The Modern, Rational Enterprise

Max Weber is in this regard very explicit: "The 'instinct of Profit,' the 'thirst for gain,' of monetary gain, indeed the maximum monetary gain possible; all this has nothing to do with capitalism. This aspiration is present and has always been present as regards waiters, doctors, coachmen, artists, prostitutes, corrupt employees, soldiers, bandits, crusaders, gamblers, beggars—it is present, one may say, amongst *all sorts and conditions of men* . . . . This ingenuous definition of the concept of capitalism must be abandoned once and for all to the primitive stage of the history of culture. The unbridled thirst for profit is not minimally identified with capitalism, and even less with its 'spirit.' Capitalism, indeed, can coincide with the modification or at least the rational control of these irrational impulses."[4]

The capitalist order in the proper sense presupposes, according to Weber, the modern, rational enterprise of a stable kind, capable of a calculation concerning capital in monetary terms and a seeking for profit as a basic condition for survival, based on an organization of labor which is formally free (a characteristic unique and exclusive to the West), on the clean separation of domestic administration and the enterprise (and in this sense work at home remains as a typically pre- or paleo-capitalist characteristic), and finally, on rational accountability.

The rise of this social structure would, however, have been impossible—and especially the assertion of a bourgeois industrial capitalism, leaving aside scientific discoveries and technical innovations—without what in Weber's view is its basic characteristic: that is to say, without rational organization of free labor. On the other hand, this characteristic, which elsewhere remained in its potential state, was fully developed in the West, thanks to the "rational structure of law and administration." "Modern rational entrepreneurial capitalism," Weber explains, "in fact needs, as well as technical instruments of production which permit calculation of forecasts, also a juridical system based on the certainty of law and an administration based on formal rules."[5] Such certainty of law and administration have only been put to the service of economic activity in the West. Why? Weber's question is a precise one. From where does this law spring? The response of ingenuous historical materialism, or mechanistic Marxism, may be guessed: this law is the reflection of those economic interests that are dominant. This is a too easy and clearly inadequate response. Weber's reply has a quite different emphasis. "In other circumstances ... *even* capitalist interests on their part have smoothed the way—even if certainly not alone, and not even as a main element—to the domination in the field of justice and administration—of a class of jurists specialized in national law. However, these interests have not *created* this law. Quite other forces have had an active role in this development. Why did capitalist interests not have the same role in China or in India? For what reason did neither scientific development, nor artistic, nor political, nor economic development open up there the path of rationalization which is peculiar to the West?"[6]

Weber's deep purpose is implicit in this question: to seek in these comparative studies, and after having tried to establish the nexus between the Protestant ethic as everyday behavior and the formation of the "spirit" or *ethos* or prevalent mentality of capitalism, to demonstrate the existence of a meaningful correlation between the precepts of an ethico-religious system as they are perceived and lived, and the specific development of economic behavior. In particular his purpose was to seek "with a general view of the relations running between the most important religions, economic life, and the social stratification of their environment; to examine the causal relations to the extent necessary to uncover the points of resemblance of Western development."[7] Thus, for Weber it was not a question of placing a priori the economic ethics as a one-sided causal framework of economic behavior and the "spirit" that inspires it and ultimately explains it, but rather to consider the interaction or bidirectional relation, which is at once cause and effect, and which in actual historical experience binds together ethics and economics, structure and personality, religion and practical interests.

3. The Social as Globality

The greatness and lasting value of Max Weber as a sociologist rest fundamentally on the quality of his research, a quality that which, it seems, cannot be reduced simply to an erudite *tour de force*, such as is all too frequently encountered in the history of sociological thought, even in recent times—the names of Vilfredo Pareto and Pitirim A. Sorokin immediately come to mind. Weber's research instead underlines a systematic effort to describe and place the constituents of the social as globality, and the careful reader will certainly not overlook the eloquent witness of this in the following pages. It is clear that the correlations found by Weber in the tangle of actual historical experience could not count on such direct research tools as the questionnaire, participant observation, or life histories, although Weber showed in his inquiry into the conditions of life of the peasants east of the Elba, that he could use these with exceptional skill. At the same time, however, his turning to *The Aubobiography of Benjamin Franklin* as the emblematic example of the new spirit of a whole epoch inserts a powerful current of methodological and substantial renewal into traditional historiography still tied to history as artistic insight and the narration of the deeds of great men, and incapable—or reluctant—to use those sociological categories, descriptive and explanatory, which would have opened the world's eyes to the social, cultural, and economic aspects which are at the basis, and which form the connecting web of great events.

To those who have always before them Weber's deepest purpose, his statement will not be unexpected: "No economic ethic is ever uniquely determined by religious factors. Each, naturally, has a level of pure autonomy, mostly determined by geographic-economic and historical data, which contrasts it to all the attitudes of man towards the world which are determined by religious or other internal (in that sense) factors. However, amongst the factors which determine economic ethics there is also—n.b.: this concerns *one* of the factors—the religious determination of the mode of life. However, this clearly, within given geographical and political, social and national frontiers, is in turn strongly influenced by economic and political factors."[8] And that Weber did not intend this to remain an abstract program, but on the contrary, to function as a basic, directing, methodological criterion of research is shown by a multitude of examples.

For instance, dealing with ancient Judaism and especially with the importance of the concept of the covenant for Israel—an importance which for Weber is linked with the ancient social system of Israel, based on a contractually defined relationship between the warrior families, the owners of land, and the guest tribes with the status of juridically protected *metoikoi*—Weber observes that "the appearance of this process does not correspond to the idea according to which the conditions of life of the Bedouins and of semi-nomads was supposed to have "produced" the foundation of orders, as the "ideological exponent" of their conditions of existence. This type of historical materialist construct is as inadequate here as elsewhere. On the other hand, it is correct to say that if this type of foundation occurred it would also have had, given the conditions of life of these strata, much greater *probabilities* of survival in the course of the struggle of selection over other, more fragile, political forms. However, its very birth depended on extremely concrete historico-religious circumstances, and often stemmed from highly personal matters."[9]

Here is sketched out the famous reciprocal reaction, the *umwälzende Praxis* of which Engels spoke, of the ideological and extraeconomic elements and all the personal qualities and biographical matters in the socioeconomic base. This "base" must never be imagined as a kind of deus ex *machina*, and its relation with the so-called superstructure must be understood as preeminent only in a very relative sense, so that not only is the "superstructure" capable of reciprocal or "dialectical" reaction on the "structure," but it furthermore is able to develop, in its own terms dialectical connections. In fact, Weber continues, pursuing the strand of religious circumstances and personal affairs, "The efficiency of the religious brotherhood as a means of political and economic power was attempted and recognized, and then naturally there followed considerable expansion of this very means. Mahomet's prophesying, like that of Jonadav Ben Rekab, cannot be 'explained' as the product of demographic and economic conditions, however much their content might also have been co-determined by these. They were rather the expression of personal experiences and aims. However, the spiritual and social means of which they availed themselves—apart from the fact of the great *success* achieved precisely by this kind of expression—are the elements explainable in the light of the conditions of life in question."[10]

If methodological shrewdness had stopped at this point, this would already be noteworthy in itself. We would find ourselves in the presence of a brilliant and essentially successful attempt to go beyond both the ingenuous view of Marxism, which confines it to the borders of vulgar materialism, and the abstract dialectical notion, which preaches dialectical relationship but does not undertake the limited historical investigations which would allow the empty, and thus far, mystifying form of that relation to be filled out with specific historical content. Weber, however, takes a still more decisive step forward. With extreme awareness, he poses the problems of the *globality* of the analysis.

4. The Interconnection Between Phenomena

If economic ethics is important for the development or the blocking of specific forms of economic behavior, Weber correctly warns that this importance also involves other spheres which are apparently distant or less immediately attainable through the terms of the problematic relationship between religion and economics. "If the ethic of religious brotherhood," Weber says in his admirable *Intermediate Observations*, "lives in a state of tension with the autonomy of rational, worldly action regarding an end, the same thing happens no less through its relations with those worldly forces of life whose essence is basically of an a- or anti-rational character: especially as regards the aesthetic and erotic sphere."[11]

It is in this ability to discover connections and grasp the substance and meaning of the most remote interconnection between phenomena, which to common sense appear different and distant, that sociological work properly exists. And it is precisely thanks to such interconnection that sociological explanation is a conditional more than a causal explanation. In other words, it is an explanation that reconstructs the significance of the social by reconnecting it and totalizing its aspects, which empirically appear fragmentary, fortuitous, and disconnected.

For a clear example of this, there is Weber's explanation of "castes and traditionalism" in India. Why did India only know through British intervention, and always with difficulty, the development of rational modern capitalism? "Karl Marx," Weber notes—and it is one of the few times when Marx is directly quoted—"identified in the peculiar position of the Indian village artisan, who works for a return fixed in nature rather than through sale on the market, the reason for the special "stability of the Asian peoples." In this he was right. . . . [however] one must take into consideration not only the position of the village artisan but also the caste system as a whole as a mainstay of this stability. Here, the result should not be understood in too direct a manner. For example, one might think that the ritualist antagonisms of the castes might have made impossible the rise of the "great enterprise" with division of labor in a single establishment, and this would have been the decisive factor. However, it is not like that. The law of the castes was shown to be flexible in the face of the needs of concentration of work in factories, as it was in the face of the need to concentrate labor and service in the castes of noble families. . . . In the same way, the laboratory, *(ergastérion)*, was considered pure. Consequently, the employee surrounded by different castes in the same workroom would not have encountered ritual obstacles, just as the proscription of interest as such in the Middle Ages did not prevent the development of industrial capital. . . . The nub of the problem did not lie in these specific difficulties. . . . The real obstacle was the "spirit" of the whole system. . . . It must appear as the summit of the unlikely, that on the basis of the caste system could ever from the beginning be *born* the modern organizational form of industrial capitalism. A ritual law on the basis of which every change of profession and working technique could lead to ritual degradation was certainly not suitable to promote economic and technical revolutions in its sphere, nor to make possible even merely the first germination of such changes. The traditionalism of the artisan, already in itself very strong, was exacerbated by this system. . . . The merchants themselves, in their ritual segregation, stayed in the fetters of the typical Eastern merchant class which has never by itself created a modern, capitalist organization of labor."[12] There is no question but that the interconnections that Weber advances and invokes as an explanation of specific historical phenomena are still too broad—that is to say, they are couched in categories like "stability," "traditionalism," "rationality," and so forth—and also too wide not to give rise to at least the suspicion that they have been adapted to cover historical and social situations which in reality do not correspond or which indeed are often not even similar. Weber is conscious of this danger and openly draws attention to it: "A great quantity of possible relations emerge before us, presented in a confused manner. . . . Our task therefore must be that of formulating what is now confusedly dancing before us with as much clarity as is allowed by the inexhaustible variety which lies in every historical phenomenon. But to do this one must necessarily abandon the field of vague general conceptions. . . . and one must try to penetrate the individual characteristics and differences of those immense worlds of religious thought. . . ."[13]

Furthermore, Weber was aware of the danger of parascientific approximations and eclectic confusions when one is concerned with linking together in a single theoretical framework, and organizing this so as to test the hypothesis, the data relating to whole historical contexts and periods of evolution which span entire epochs, whose simple description itself involves an exceptional philological commitment.

5. The Problem of Method

These observations should not make the reader think that with Weber we are faced with a formalist methodologist of a type that today is highly common. Weber knew that the problem of method is basic, and had in any case dedicated to it long periods of meditation and articles which in some ways are still decisive today. However, he also knew that the method and the object of inquiry cannot be separated, that the function of method cannot be clarified in a problematic void, that the idea of being able equally to apply to any object of inquiry a method set out and defined from the technical point of view is a fatal illusion for sociology, in that it means indifference regarding themes of research and hence a fall into arbitrary methodologism.[14]

Weber often returned to the bidirectional character of his research: "The question posed in the first instance is . . . that of recognizing the distinctive characteristics of Western rationalism and, within this, the outlines of its modern form, and then of explaining its origin. Every explanatory study of this kind, *bearing in mind the basic importance of the economic factor,* must take into consideration first of all the economic conditions. *But the inverse correlation also should not be left to one side.*"[15] Probing into the treatment of the problem, Weber was afraid of falling victim to the customary misinterpretation which mistakes problematic awareness and the precise definition of the object of research with the normative evaluation that transforms any typological directory into a scale of priorities from the point of view of value.

He said, "The scheme which is constructed has *naturally the sole aim of being an ideal-typical instrument for orientation, not for teaching a particular philosophy.*"[16]

This must have preoccupied Weber a great deal, as he rigorously stresses this particular point, offering the reader the mechanical elements, as it were, or the technique of ideal-typical construction in the light of the elaboration of a typology able to direct research through the undergrowth of empirical data, and at the same time to guarantee the possibility of establishing a whole series of plausible interconnections, even if these are not absolutely proved from the point of view of empirical warranties. "The types of 'orders of living' in conflict which are theoretically constructed, simply demonstrate that in these places (China, India, etc.) these conflicts are possible and 'sufficient'—but one does not exclude the existence of points of view from which these conflicts may be considered 'overcome.' One can easily see how the individual spheres of values are elaborated into an organic, rational structure such as rarely exists in reality, even if they can be realized and in fact have been realized historically in important forms. This construction, in the presence of a historical phenomenon which in certain aspects and by way of its global character, approaches one of these forms, *makes it possible to identify its typological position by ascertaining the level of closeness to or distance from the theoretically constructed type.*"[17]

6. Method as a Reflection on Work

We have, however, already noted in Weber's methodological comments an element of impatience. He is ready to immerse himself and to come to terms with specific historical, cultural, and social situations—that is, to explain his method by practising it in the living process of research, and to let it be known that basically for him methodological questions are simply *reflections on work during work itself,* the thinking aloud of a tireless intellectual artisan. Simple concentration on method independent of content—or more precisely, by neglecting as a secondary dimension of research specific problematic awareness—is one of the most certain signs of decadence in sociological thought, the symptom of a separation already occurring between concepts and techniques of research, and hence the inevitable impoverishment of both. Obviously, this does not mean mistaking the importance of method. It only means recognizing the dialectical nature, the historical nature, of sociological concepts that must therefore be constructed and weighed in the scale of historically mature and emerging problems in relation to specific historical contexts. At the same time it must not be forgotten that the object of sociology is not in itself sociology, but rather, social problems—that is to say, those problematic human situations which are pointed out not by the market, nor by more or less farsighted customers, but rather by the internal logic of research itself, which thereby presents itself as the ultimate guarantee of the autonomy of sociological judgment.

This autonomy is not absolute. On the contrary, it is *directly related to the historical self-placement of the researcher.* In this delicate operation of self-placement, or in the conscious choice of an explicit point of view—which implies renouncing the naturalistic type of objectivity and at the same time embracing the frank recognition that every attempt on the researcher's part to place himself above the parties historically at issue, freely floating above material interests and the principled taking of positions, in reality, means and involves condemnation to irrelevance— in this, there properly lies "historical consciousness." This necessarily further implies the recognition of the relativity of every point of view, not in the sense of an absolute relativism which would coincide with a universal skeptical position and moral indifference, but rather in the sense that every point of view—even that most plausibly established— cannot refuse to open itself to the problematic question without freezing itself into a dogma, and thus without denying itself precisely as a point of view linked to a "historical consciousness" given and experienced, and not in a contradictory way hypostasized as an eternal, metahistorical form.

One cannot say that Weber resolved this group of problems, which is exceptionally difficult, especially in regard to the relationship between knowing and evaluating, and the equally controversial one between intellectual lucidity and practicopolitical decisions which in the traditional Marxist literature is hastily identified as the problem of the relationship between theory and practice. What one can with a fair degree of certainty assert is that method for Weber is secondary: as it was for Marx, for Thorstein Veblen, and for all the great sociologists of the classic epoch of sociology.

For these sociologists, the task of research did not lie in navel-gazing and concentrating on oneself in an intimate activity of listening to one's own body rhythms. Sociology was in the first place, basically, an instrument for taking account of the historical situation in which they were living, its basic characteristics, and the probable developments which, on the basis of the latter, one could correctly *hypothesize*. For them, sociology was *thus the science of the historical social movement and the direction and meaning of this movement*. Sociological theory and society thus did not confront each other as external, counterposed realities. Theory lay within society: it constantly questioned it and was continuously called to account by it. It followed it and went before it as its inseparable shadow.

In this sense, there is a hidden danger of misunderstanding in the now customary formulation of Weber's argument, which reduces it to the critical examination of the relations between religion and society. This same misunderstanding of Weber's thought in the sense of vulgar anti-Marxism is in this perspective a clear warning of danger. Religion and society are not in fact separate worlds, nor should they be crudely conceived of as separate spheres. Religion, like economics, culture, politics, and so forth, is a social fact. Religion and society have in common the basic fact of being two social realities, of pointing to two realities which are not only analogous or homologous or assimilable, or in various ways interactive, but rather of both being social experiences, historical moments of the sociality of the social.

7. Beyond Intellectualist Schematism

One must thus avoid counterposing elements based—rather than on an attempt at genuine conceptualization (that is to say, the attempt conceptually to organize a series of empirical data)—on videogames of intellectualist schematism which spiral around themselves and pay for their ultimate formal elegance with an unbridgeable distance in regard to reality. Certainly Weber was aware of and describes the tensions that run between a religious ethic of brotherhood and the functional requirements of a rational, modern capitalist economy and the structure of a modern political state. "A rational economy," he states, "is a functional activity. It is based on monetary prices which originate from the struggle of interests of men in the market. Without estimates in monetary prices, and hence without this struggle of interests, there is no possible estimate of any kind. Money is the most abstract and "impersonal" thing which exists in the life of man. Consequently, the more the world of modern, rational capitalist economics followed its immanent laws, *so, increasingly, it became inaccessible to any relation with a religious ethic of brotherhood.* This distance grew with the growth of rationality and impersonality. Indeed, an integral ethical regulation of the personal relation between master and slave was possible precisely because this involved a personal relationship. On the other hand, it was not possible . . . to regulate relations between the owners—always diverse—of the holders of debts and the borrowers of loans from the bank, each unknown to the other and interchangeable, between which there was no type of personal bond."[18]

Weber offers an analogous argument regarding modern political structures: "The idea of brotherhood in the religions of redemption, if logical, should also find itself in a state of specially acute tension as regards the political orders of the world. For magical religiosity, as for that of functional gods, the problem did not exist . . . (however, the basic element of every political society is the appeal to naked violence as a means of coercion, not only towards the outside but also towards the inside. Indeed, violence is that which in our terminology defines, in the first instance, political society. The "state" is the association which claims the monopoly of the legitimate use of violence—there are no other definitions. . . . Every politics will thus be the more extraneous to brotherhood as it is "objective" and calculating, free from aroused sentiments, without anger and without love. The reciprocal extraneousness of the two spheres of politics and etics, when both are completely rationalised, is shown with especial harshness on decisive points, *insofar as politics, as against economics, is able to present itself as a direct competitor of religious ethics*."[19]

8. Marx and Weber: An Existential Convergence

In Weber's terms, then, this is a question of the tension between two spheres, the religious and the economicopolitical, but not of a contraposition with the subsequent mutual exclusion between society and religion. Rather, and with greater clarity, we are faced with the integration of two situations, one of which is religious and the other extrareligious, or worldly, profane, but both of which *at the same time are social situations.* For this reason, the global outlook of the investigation and the search for interconnections not readily visible to the eye of common sense become important moments of sociological research, to the point of constituting its essence and typical method of procedure. Here Marx and Weber demonstrate a clear tendency to coincide. Nor is this only a question of existential convergences determined by the common German cultural framework, and by the fact that we are dealing with two characters of a personal morality and typically Victorian, respectable, temperamental reactions—all in all, very much aware of being *Herr Professor* in a time and place in which the professor is still a demigod, not reduced to a functionary. Separated by a crucial couple of generations, both had studied in Berlin: both believed in the work ethic and practised it—Marx at the British Museum and Weber at home for reasons of nervous prostration—with a superhuman determination. As for the Victorian, respectable Puritanism, it is enough to think of Marx's anguish regarding his bastard son and the tormented relationship between Weber and his mother, possibly not without having a bearing on the tragic mysterious death of his father. It is not simply a matter of this—which obviously has its own importance. We are dealing with a convergence of method and substance which leads to impressive analytical consequences.

See the passage in which Weber, analyzing Confucianism and Taoism, is struck by their basic anti-individualism and observes that "neither here nor in Egypt nor in Mesopotamia did military cavalry technique ever lead to a social interconnection as individualistic as in the 'Homeric' Hellas, and in the 'Middle Ages.'"[20] The explanatory factor of this anti-individualism, or lack of individualism, was not sought either in ethics or in psychology or in the sociopolitical system. Rather, the interconnection is made by way of a joint phenomenon of a geographical and technological nature: The inevitable dependence of the whole population on the regulation of watercourses, and hence the total subordination to the personal bureaucratic government of the prince "acted as a counterweight."

Here in a nutshell is the whole "hydraulic theory of oriental despotism" of Karl Wittfogel, but these observations by Weber also recall the article published by Marx in the *New York Herald Tribune* regarding the rationalizing and antitraditional effects exerted by the railroad built in India by the English on a static and technically archaic social system. In addition, the structure of Weber's reasoning is not dissimilar from that of Marx in the first book of *Das Kapital*, where in those wonderful chapters devoted to the coming of great mechanized industry and the working day—so rich in technical detail and so accurate in their description of the productive process as to make one suspect a direct contribution from Engels and the benefits of his personal experience as director of general production in the family textile firm in Manchester—Marx magisterially reconstructs the framework and conditions of the breakup of the working-class family through a series of interconnections which start from an innocent technical innovation—the incorporation of the tool in the machine. This technical innovation, seemingly neutral, in reality has a dual order of consequences. On the one hand, it specializes the machine while it dequalifies the worker. The artisan of times past, now a worker after losing his property (that is, the legal control of his means of production), now also loses control of the disposition of his nervous and muscular strength, and his sense of direct responsibility regarding his work, insofar as it no longer depends on him to decide the inclination of the tool in the cutting of the raw material, and hence the machine's cutting speed, and hence the time of production. On the other hand, the incorporation of the tool into the machine makes possible the hiring on a stable basis of less qualified female working power—though qualification is no longer an essential requirement now that the machine has been "promoted,"—but providing a more docile labor force. The women thus abandon their home and children, and replace their men in the workplace. The latter find themselves with nothing to do and resort to alcohol. With a characteristic absence of proletarian sentimentalism, Marx notes that the male workers, along with this technical innovation, see their family break up, begin to take to drink, and sell on the capitalist labor market, formerly free, their wives and children; they become, Marx concludes, the "new slave traders."

It should not be unusually surprising that this extraordinary ability to grasp meaningful interconnections should allow Marx—and also Weber—startling foresights which have, in retrospect for us, an almost prophetic value. I am not thinking of the so-called Messianism of Marx, which, above all when it is connected with the Jewish cultural matrix, or more precisely, Marx's biblical connections, I can only consider with irreconcilable distaste. Rather, I am thinking of the scientific foresight of Marx relation to industrial gigantism, to the growth of the industrial proletariat, which was scarcely beginning in Marx's time, the vision of industrialized society as class society, dichotomously cut up and divided between those who possess the means of production and those who are possessed by it; that is, between owners and expropriated. Even if in the short term this dichotomous vision of society seems to be denied by immediate facts, so great is the proliferation of strata and intermediate quasi classes, there seems to be no doubt that in the long term a tendential bipolarity is being marked out, in terms of power, destined to delineate in a basic fashion the class structure of technically advanced societies.

Welcome surprises of this kind, possibly more limited and from a linguistic point of view less flirtatious with the ground of Hegel's argument, are, however, often to be found in Weber also. For example, on the basis of a resemblance of the organization of landed property between China and Russia, we see in Weber an extraordinary, prophetic insight: "The, so to speak, "effective" peasants . . . were thus quite typically at the mercy of the decisions of the *Kung kun,* the Kulaks ("fists") as they would be called in Russian peasant terminology . . . the peasants had to deal with the "propertyless" organized by each *Kung kun,* that is, with the "bédnate" ("village poverty") in the real sense of the terminology of Bolshevism, *which would have been able to find precisely in this the basis of its force of attraction for China.*"[21] Perhaps only in Thorstein Veblen, in his book *Imperial Germany and the Industrial Revolution,*[22] where, on the basis of a fiercely detached description of the "sporting propensities of the masses" of today, including the working class, he theorizes on the possibility of the capture of the "loyalty" of these masses on the part of some Führer sufficiently skillful in the art of mystification, do we have an analogous example of predictive insight.

When, however, Weber had to provide a basis for his own encyclopedic knowledge, he did not, alongside a reference to the *Veda* or the reading of biblical texts or Calvin's *Institutes,* disdain at times to make use of quotations from newspaper articles; and in this also, the similarity with Marx is striking. Just as Marx quotes from the *Morning Star* of the June 23,

1863, in *Das Kapital*,[23] the news regarding the "death from work," of the young textile worker Mary Anne Walkley, so Weber had no hesitation in supporting his argument on the importance of the Tongs in China by quoting from the *Peking Gazette* of April 14, 1895, regarding the "liberation by two associations of *Tongs*, of an individual arrested by a tax collector."[24] This is a tradition, the sociological use of quotations from newspapers, which was far from unworthily continued by Vilfredo Pareto and without serious shock continued into Herbert Marcuse's *One-Dimensional Man*.

9. Toward a Unitary Science of Man in Society

From Weber, therefore, as from Marx, there comes a strong impulsion toward the elaboration of a unitary science of man in society. This is a global outlook for research that goes beyond the scholastic and merely instrumental conception of the interdisciplinary approach, which is thus reduced to a simple artifice to guarantee the division of academic work, splitting up the tendentially unitary character of sociological research in regard to specific problems. It is clear, however, and hardly necessary in the case of Weber to draw attention to the fact that the relative needs of unitariness and globality should not be understood as a kind of non-admitted indulgence to generalizing vagueness and theoretical lack of precision.

It is particularly in *The Protestant Ethic and the Spirit of Capitalism* that Weber deliberately tried to tighten up, as it were, his argument, which he was the first to see as an argument made with an excessively large mesh, with references and contrasts between one civilization and another, because of the breadth and multidimensionality of his research project. There is no doubt that in regard to Christianity—and hence the relationship between Catholicism and Protestantism, and thence within the latter the Protestant sects from Calvinism to Pietism, to Methodism and the Baptist movement—Weber proposes to go into detail. He notes the necessity of a more rigorous logicolinguistic specification of the terms employed, and basically anticipates the remarks of his most formidable critic, Kurt Samuelsson: "Weber's hypothesis of a direct correlation between Puritanism and economic progress is a generalization which, aside from the problem of its factual groundedness, is methodologically inadmissible. The two phenomena are so vague and universal as not to be open to an evaluation through the technique of correlation."[25]

We have already remarked on these methodological difficulties in the strict sense, difficulties which are real but are, however, not such, in my view, as to weaken the conceptual bases and general design of Weber's project—the more so as the analysis of world religions carried out by Weber is important in its design only as an indirect testing of the analysis that he proposed to carry out on the forms of Christian ethics, understood not as "a theological theory" but as "an impulsion to action" in relation to the development of modern, rational capitalism and especially its "spirit."[26]

What, however, is "the spirit of capitalism"? (At the word *Geist* [spirit], Schopenhauer used to ask,*"Wer ist der Bursche."* [And who is this young fellow?]). Weber argues: "The perfect conceptual definition cannot . . . stand at the head, but must be placed at the finish, of the investigation. It will thus reveal itself in the course of the treatment, and the important conclusion will be how best to formulate, most adequately for the points of view which interest us here, that which we understand as the 'spirit of capitalism.'"[27]

Little by little, the elements characteristic of this key concept emerge from Weber's pages: reasonable utilitarianism; the thirst for profit, tempered by rationality and above all by honesty, seen instrumentally not so much a value in itself as the means by which to obtain financial credit; antitraditionalism; and finally the concept of "profession" in its double meaning of "working activity" and "religious vocation," which it would be "pure stupidity" to consider as the simple reflection of material conditions. According to Weber, this concept of *Beruf* is the one on which any scientific explanation of the genesis of modern capitalist must hinge. As against the conception of Werner Sombart, who sees the origins of modern capitalism simplistically in "satisfaction of needs" and "profit," Weber finds that in the ethic lived out by the Protestant sects, "there was one completely new thing: the evaluation of the fulfillment of one's own duty, in the worldly professions, as the highest form which ethical activity can take."[29] The practical consequences of this "absolute novelty" do not escape Weber: "Thus, in the concept of *Beruf,* the central dogma of all Protestant denominations finds expression; the dogma which rejects the Catholic distinction of the ethical commandments of Christianity into *praecepta* and *consilia*, and which recognizes as the only method of living in a manner which finds favor in God, not transcendence through the monkly asceticism of the morals of those who live in the world, but exclusively the fulfillment of one's own worldly duties, as these are presented by the position of each in life."[30]

In many ways, ideal and practicopolitical, Lutheranism and Catholicism are counterposed; but they find themselves once again united in common opposition to Calvinism, the "historical representative of ascetic Protestantism," in which Weber recognizes a determining function in the creation of the modern capitalist spirit. Naturally, the reasons for attrition between Lutherans and Roman Catholics on the one hand and Calvinists on the other, are numerous. "However, the basis of the aversion towards Calvinism common to Catholics and Lutherans," Weber notes, "is also to be found in the ethical character of Calvinism. Even the most superficial observation shows us that the latter had set up a relation between religious life and profane action of a completely different kind to that which we find in Catholicism, and equally in Lutheranism."[31] Indeed, it is on Calvinism that Weber sees depending the double acceptance—or the simultaneous religious and profane scope of the concept of *Beruf*. On the other hand, understandably, it is on this concept that the fire of anti-Weberian criticisms are centered.

10. The Critics of Weber's Thesis

The long list of critics starts with H. M. Robertson, who unites in the same polemic an attack on both Weber and R. H. Tawney, aligning himself instead with Lujo Brentano, the celebrated colleague of Weber—a member of an old banking family of Italian and Catholic origin—who did not hesitate to call upon that background as evidence against Weber's argument.[32] Far from recognizing an important function in the concept and practice of *Beruf* as regards the advent of modern rational capitalism, Robertson is rather inclined to attribute this function to the "geographical discoveries" as prime causes of the displacement of cconomic and commercial activity toward the Protestant countries, to the detriment of the Mediterranean and Roman Catholic countries.[33] During the same period, Amintore Fanfani and a host of other minor critics tried to demonstrate the deficiency of Weber's argument, simply by asserting that the "spirit" of capitalism and the lived ethics, or the religious spirit irrespective of denomination, had nothing in common, and thus had nothing to share. This is a peculiar resolution of the problem, which essentially arrives at its pure and simple suppression.[34] The only extenuating circumstance, perhaps, was provided by the research by W. Cunningham — earlier by some years than that of Weber—who did not even mention Calvinism and who saw in the process of secularization rather than in any religious ethic the basic factor which had prepared the way for the development of individualistic and rational capitalism in the modern era.[35]

The concept of *Beruf*, however, which is difficult to undermine on the properly theoretic level—instead offers its flank to criticisms that seem to me well-based when, as is done explicitly by Weber, this concept is fleshed out in the person of Benjamin Franklin. It is certainly difficult to demonstrate an even nearly remotely religious character in Franklin's personality. In fact, one cannot imagine a human and social type further from the wholly Calvinistic activism and concern, providing himself with the largest possible number of guarantees of the *certitudo salutis* in the light of the theology of predestination of this Philadelphia gentleman—naturally aristocratic, a diplomat and traveler and hopelessly infatuated with good classical literature and mature ladies ("they are so grateful"!), who dreams only of saving enough to be able to retire, to go for walks, and study in a house full of books and a garden full of flowers. Indeed, I feel that from Weber's point of view, Benjamin Franklin, one of the Founding Fathers and ambassador to Paris for the new-fledged United States, inventor of the lightning rod and darling of the women, is a mistaken choice for hero. One is led to think that here Weber projected his religious anxieties, repressed at the back of his consciousness, onto a pragmatic character who has none of his suffering, an agnostic and peaceful as only a Deist can be—the atheists are the only ones to be seriously concerned about God.

Less convincing do I find the criticisms directed at Weber on the basis of the fact that at least a hundred years before Benjamin Franklin, a Frenchman—a Catholic moreover, Jacques Savary—published a book in which one can find ideas and advice not dissimilar to those proposed by Franklin.[36] Samuelsson and Lüthy make much of Savary, a protoutilitarian and protorepresentative of "the spirit of capitalism."[37]

For his part, Werner Sombart finds a forerunner of Benjamin Franklin in Leon Battista Alberti, and in *Der Bourgeois* he quotes extensively from *I libri della famiglia*. Sombart, too, in his major work *Modern Capitalism*[38] selects as the authentic representative of "the capitalist spirit"—and in any case one more genuine than the hero selected by Weber—the great financier Jakob Fugger, who was endowed with a sporting taste for amassing money and was naturally never ready for retirement. Weber took Sombart's remarks very seriously and devoted a long footnote to the question of the relationship between Alberti and Franklin.

In fact, for Weber's argument, it was less important to establish the philological precedents of a particular philosophico-practical position than to determine the representative nature of the exemplary or emblematic type selected as the personification of the new, emerging mentality. From this point of view, notwithstanding Weber's errors in interpretation, Franklin probably has a higher value of representativeness than the other forerunners mentioned by the critics.[39]

In other words, I am saying that Weber's argument cannot be refuted merely on the basis of some inexactitude of detail or in terms of some philosophical, philological oversight. The latter, given the encyclopedic nature of his work, is a possibility which is wholly realistic. One has to bear in mind Weber's intention and the average level of generalization on which his argument is based. Even if Savary lived a hundred years before Franklin—and perhaps precisely for that reason—it is probable that Franklin would have a representative value regarding the predominant or average mentality which is markedly higher than that of Savary or Alberti or even Jakob Fugger.[40]

A similar argument can be made about the criticisms of the slender conceptual accuracy that Weber was to exhibit in setting out the theological doctrines of the representatives of ascetic Protestantism. A critique of this sort has been made by, among others, Carlo Antoni in the revealing profile that he devotes to Weber in the book *Dallo storicismo alla sociologia*.[41] This is a critique which demonstrates in its author a serious misunderstanding. Weber's intention does not lie in a discussion of theology at a high level of abstraction. He is not concerned with a philosophical discussion of pure ethics. For the purposes of his research, what interests him is not so much the ethical thought of Protestant theologians as the average moral sense—that is to say, the "lived ethic," or the ethic that is reflected in daily behavior, interpersonal relations, economic activity, or commercial transaction. For this reason, rather than in the Institutes of Calvin, Weber is interested in the *Christian Directory* of Richard Baxter; that is to say, in theological theory, but only insofar as it becomes an impulsion to action, the practice of life, the rule of conduct.[42] I can understand in this regard the disappointment of a refined historian of philosophy or the frustrations of a philologist, but I must not forget that Weber intended otherwise.

CHAPTER FIVE

THE MODERN WORLD AND ITS DESTINY:
From "Disenchantment" to "Steel Cage"

1. The Problem

For the lasting, even growing reputation of Max Weber as man and thinker, there are at least two reasons. First, there is an essential reason: Weber tackles a central theme, one that is still today at the heart of our concerns, and to which he returns in all his works, more or less directly — the nature, direction, and future of the modern world. Then, second, there is the method whereby this theme is set out and analyzed, which concerns method in the wide sense of the word, including the theoretical-conceptual apparatus and specific research techniques.

What is, for Weber, the modern world? It is a world ruled and defined by "rational calculation." In Weber's perspective, the modern world is one of *total calculability*. The construction of this modern world as one rationally "calculated" or "calculable" passes through two basic phases: (1) "disenchantment" *(Entzauberung der Welt);* and (2) the laicization and routinization of *Beruf* ("vocation"), which becomes mundane as a specific bureaucratic-methodical competence, instead of being a calling, or religious vocation.

It seems hardly necessary to note that this two-layered process of social transformation takes place and develops in the framework of a still more radical shift — a real historical leap — wherein we have a transition from a magicoreligious traditionalism, a vision of human destiny that is essentially transcendent, of which we might say with Goethe that *"Alles Vergangliche/ ist nur ein Gleichnis."* We proceed to a society characterized by a process of increasingly large-scale industrialization, with the openly declared intention of producing its own values, and which furthermore does not acknowledge the binding force of any criterion of evaluation outside the internal correctness of its own proceedings. Once transcendence has collapsed, or more exactly, once transcendent principles have been translated and reduced to methodical daily habits (at the root of which Weber sometimes seems to continue to perceive the glimmer of ancient religious values, no longer consciously grasped or accepted as such), Weber's modern world seems to be in a Nietzschian sense "human, all too human."

The contrast with types of preceding societies—traditional, paleotechnical, preindustrial—all linked to a marked, all-pervasive, magicoreligious symbolism, is so strong as to be presented as a qualitative break. As Huizinga, for example, comments, "The spirit of that time was so full of Christ that the slimmest analogy with the Lord's life or passion which any act or thought might have, would instantly summon up his image. A poor nun bringing firewood into the kitchen saw herself as bearing the Cross. The simple idea of bearing wood was enough to surround the action with the aura of a supreme act of love. A blind washerwoman takes the wash-tub and wash-board for the crib and stable."[1]

2. From the Magicoreligious to the Individualized Rational

In the modern world, there is no longer room for this magicoreligious, essentially other-worldly symbolism. In Weber's view, at the most it exists in a residual space, necessarily destined to disappear. The "sense," the meaning, of the modern, rational, individualized world can develop only in inverse proportions to the gradual withdrawal, the so-to-speak contraction of the magicoreligious sphere. Indeed, as Weber says in *Economy and Society*, "The more intellectualism rejects belief in magic, and thus the processes of the world become 'disenchanted' *(und so die Vorgänge der Welt 'entzaubert' werden)*, they lose their magical meaning; they are restricted to 'being' and 'appearing' *(geschehen)*, instead of 'meaning' *(bedeuten)*, so the need increases for the world, the 'conduct of life' *Lebensführung)*, insofar as they make up a whole, to be meaningfully set out and 'provided with meaning' *(sinnvoll)*."[2]

In his usual meticulous manner, Weber analyzes the "paths" whereby "intellectualism"—first of all, responsible for "disenchantment"—gradually becomes a current, shared idea, instead of being limited to narrow intellectual circles. It is the typical attitude of a whole social form and existential inclination, or an empirically testable character proclivity, of a whole historical phase. In Weber's view, the resulting collapse of "magico-religious meaning" increases and indeed makes essential the responsible adoption of "life conduct" as in itself "meaningful" *(sinnvoll)*, endowed with meaning no longer tied to transcendent symbolic meanings and collective-communitarian validity, but rather as these emphasize the moral and intellectual responsibility of the individual—only now, at last, faced with his knowledge and his God. Weber, therefore, not only makes clear the results, but primarily the premises and cultural bases of the process of industrialization, as a universal social one, which defines the modern world. He also stresses the elitist and typically intellectual nature of those bases, right from their evolutionary-genetic beginning.[3] One should not, however, thereby believe in a Weber indulgent toward a formulation of the description and interpretation—if not the explanation—of social phenomena in a monocausal sense. Nor, on the basis of the undeniable implications in certain passages taken out of context, should one support a basically "evolutionistic" Weber, as Talcott Parsons has done. This demonstrates a fundamental misunderstanding of Weber's position—which, however, had from Parson's point of view, the advantage of making Weber a kind of forerunner of "social action," as it was to be developed by the author of *The Social System* in collaboration with other sociologists and social analysts, ranging from Robert Bales to Edward A. Shils, George C. Homan, and Neil Smelser.

In Weber the analysis of the process of rationalization (which exists as one of the bases of the coming of the modern world and, in essence, defines it and makes it up), makes no concession to the theory of the "great evolutionary universals" which in Parsons's view can be identified in the growth and development of all human societies. In the same way, Weber is very careful regarding the ever-possible confusion between analytical concepts—needful for research as mental constructs for meaningfully reordering the immense mass of empirical data—and concrete historical situations, which are nonreducible in their specificity. Far from the often empty generalization which characterizes Parsons's method, with its curious identification of social theory with the simple construction of basically arbitrary, excessively generalized abstract models—to the point of tumbling into theoretical vagueness and the generic—Weber is concerned with identifying what is unique in the historical experience of the West. He strongly criticizes the evolutionary, holistic tendencies both in their cumulative and mechanistic form (Spencer), and in the historical, dialectical one (Marx).

It is easy, especially in regard to "disenchantment" and "rationalization," to acquire a misleading view of Weber's thought. Weber can be reproved for a limitation, or for a certain Nietzschean taste for the aphorism, the fragmentary, but in fact this is his great merit. It does not seem to me correct to consider this as solely the reflection of his logical philosophical position as a neo-Kantian, which excludes any generalization on the ultimate nature of the social phenomena dealt with, just as it would be hard to find in Weber the equivalent of a supraindividual reality comparable to Durkheim's *"représentations collectives."* Rather, it should be remembered that Weber always clearly distinguishes between, and keeps separate, the analytical level and the specific historic content. In his analysis of social phenomena, Weber is a rigorous individualist, applying and achieving a strictly individualist methodological approach although—far from falling into a psychologistic position or one, as has been suggested, close to "symbolic interactionism"—he was solely concerned with large institutional complexes, with a basically structuralist outlook.

We shall see later, when we look more directly at the form of Weber's method, what is implied by the contradiction we have indicated. What should be stressed here is that the concept of rationality, which for Weber underlies the process of rationalization, is in no way schematic, or intrinsically required. It is not necessarily progressive or cumulative in a unilinear sense. Indeed, it contains a multiplicity of meanings and thus is presented basically as a problematic concept.

Sociological analysis has often proceeded by means of a schematic counterposing of historically different situations and phases, nicely summarized in an umbrella concept, such as community versus society, nature versus culture, economy versus ideology, structure versus personality, tradition versus rationality, military versus industrial society, and so on. In regard to these rather mechanical, historically ingenuous dualisms, Weber's position appears much more problematic and complex, and in any case far removed from black-and-white interpretations. One can even say that he was strongly attracted by the contradictory aspects and antinomies of rationality.

In this regard, Reinhard Bendix has cited two well-known, convincing examples. As against the widespread notion that Weber's thought describes a unilinear and necessarily progressive development from a magicoreligious epoch to a historical, rationalist-scientific phase, or from a patrimonial type of economic undertaking—or one of robbery—to one based on rational calculation (written, ongoing accountability, with scientific planning of available resources in respect to profit), one should remember Weber's analysis of ancient Judaism and Calvin's teaching in the context of the Protestant ethic.[4] In the first instance, we have a decline in the magicoreligious sphere because of the rise of prophecy. As Weber accurately notes, however, after the Babylonian captivity, the dynamic power of the prophets yields and gives way to ritualized faithfulness to the law under the tutelage of the rabbis. Thus, here increasing rationality first determines, or accompanies, the broad values of a monotheist religion, only later to debouch into the irrationality of formalized rituals and the loss of interior meaning in commandments initially rich with symbolic significance. As Weber observed, "The prophetic horizon remained wholly terrestrial, like the official Babylonian one, as against the Greek mysteries and the Orphean religion. Jewish prophecy, though linked to the Levites' care of the soul, was concerned only with the destiny of the people as a whole. Thereby it repeatedly demonstrated its political orientation. The increasing bourgeois rationalism of a people integrated into the relatively pacified world of the Persian empire, and afterwards that of Hellenism, made the suppression of prophecy possible for the priests."[5]

As for Calvinism, the analytic precision with which Weber makes clear the paradox of the teaching is well known. This referred to the total inscrutability of the divine will as well as to the *certainty of salvation.* At the same time, in regard to the practical business of life or lived morality, it draws conclusions about methodical living, industry, the sanctification of life, sobriety and saving, and thus about the accumulation and subsequent reinvestment of capital. One starts with uncertainty about one's own ultratenestrial salvation and ends with the foundation of the major Swiss banks. This same brilliant nature of Weber's work has itself created an opportunity for crude misunderstanding. Even a cursory reconstruction of the cultural climate prevailing at the time of Weber's text —the beginning of the present century—may be sufficient to let us understand both its success and its deficiencies in understanding. A major success is almost always a great danger. Weber provided the example for an unusual heterogenesis of aims, in order to show the complex, multidimensional character, the basic *reciprocity* of the relation between structure and culture.[6] Weber's meticulous analytical precision, however, has not been given full credit. Bendix himself, as Eisenstadt has shown, did not explore his subject profoundly enough, being content with a cursory presentation.[7] For Weber, there was no question of overthrowing Marx's argument —or more precisely, overturning that of the Marxism of his day, mostly undialectical and as yet unaware of the *Economic and Philosophic Manuscripts of 1844,* as well as of the *Grundrisse* —but simply of exposing the complex interaction, which cannot a priori be established by a wholly theoreticodeductive calculation. It thus requires a specific historical research of the bidirectional relation between the structure of "material" and "ideal" interests.

3. The Idea of Interest

We are thus not faced with a counterposition between "material interests" and "ideas," but rather between two different types of interest. The central category, however, is always that of interest —also, what is involved in the sphere of knowledge that is not directly applicable or useful. This must be borne in mind as it helps to explain some important aspects of Weber's position:

1. His rejection of vulgar anti-Marxism and his explicit recognition of Marxism as a working hypothesis, or "ideal-type" model, albeit one among others.
2. The rejection of an all-inclusive conceptual system, tendentially, dogmatically, closed, in favor of the "open system," linked to the value choices of the individual. This gives rise to the characteristic "moderate relativism" (moderated by the major values of the European liberal tradition which, as we can boldly say today, Weber sees as *eternally* secured, and so beyond question).
3. The typically Weberian tendency not to be limited to a literally correct reading of the theological texts and the ethic of Protestantism and other religions, but rather to be concerned with a lived ethic that is, with ethical precepts as they are manifested in everyday existence

through the practical behavior of determinate individuals and social groups.

4. Finally, the profound argument dealing with universal religions, immediately relevant to our discussion in that it rests on a dual purpose. First, it attempts to establish comparatively the terms of the *uniqueness* of the historical experience of Western Europe *("Nur in Okzident . . .),* contrasted with the failure to develop capitalism in other parts of the world, governed by other ethical or religious systems, or other magicoreligious models. To these last, Weber does not attribute a necessarily causal responsibility in the literal sense for the failure of capitalist development of the West European kind, but he sees them as meaningful accompaniments. Secondly, it tries to determine the process of the beginning of rationalization, which was to peak and be diffused through the triumph of rationality as a principle of social organization and a new source of the legitimation of power by means of a series of intermediate stages which run from "disenchantment of the world" to the camouflage of religious values under fake lay dress. This is Thomas Luckmann's "invisible religion." At the other extreme these arrive at the scientifically, rationally determined work of formal bureaucratic orders and ultimately at the dubious victory of a white-collar world peopled by hard-working, malleable men and women.

What strikes one in Weber's broad and at times repetitive analysis is the precision with which he grasps and brings out the traditional elements in the innovative, rationalizing processes, and at the same time the factors of change in a rational direction already present in the structure of traditions. (Some imperfections of form are certainly to be attributed to its posthumous appearance and to the fact that it was edited by J. Winckelmann, with great fidelity to the originals.) In this perspective, it would be hard to see in Weber a kind of precursor or distinguished forerunner of the schematic theories of "secularization," and still less of the current well-known argument concerning a supposed "eclipse of the sacred." The somewhat extemporary nature of these and similar theories is clear in the connection—so much taken for granted as not to require empirical testing—between urbanization and industrialization and still more between industrialization and the scientific attitude, based on the cause-effect sequence. However, the survival in advanced industrial societies of many animistic and sometimes crudely anthropomorphic beliefs shows that acceptance of a cultural model based on rigorous rationality in a scientific sense is still sporadic and in any event liable to major exceptions.

4. Rationality as a Problematic Concept

One can plausibly argue further that the examples quoted by Weber in support of his case (especially as material proving the Protestant ethic to be a factor in industrial economic development and in "the spirit of capitalism" as a way of life) are not wholly credible. That Benjamin Franklin clearly represents a typification of the Protestant ethic in practice is somewhat dubious; likewise, or even more so, is the example of Fugger, cited by Werner Sombart, the distinguished critic and opponent of Weber. At any rate, it is not a question of this: or rather, it is not a question of accuracy or adequacy in the literal sense of the words, but rather of Weber's general conception of the nature of the modern world. In Weber's terms, this nature can be traced to the specific forms of the process of rationalization, as taken on from time to time in the different fields of the—analytically discernible—social. This process is seen in terms of a general concept of a rationality never completely or definitively stated, which varies and is transformed in the different sectors of social life, from the religious to the economic political, juridical, and organizational-bureaucratic.

Weberian rationality is thus essentially problematic. As for that Eurocentrism which, for Weber as for the scholars of his generation, is unconsciously taken as an initial premise, one might say that rationality is a unique characteristic of Western European history: at the same time, it is a normative term, a historic task to be performed, a real *Grenz-Begriff*, an idea-limit. As such, it is positive; but at the very moment that it seems to be historically achieved, and on the point of becoming dominant, it reverses itself and takes on a negative connotation in the context of a totally administered society and a tendentially totalizing bureaucratico-formal organization, which cheats the individual out of his rationality in order to set him in the name of efficiency in a "steel cage."

Weber's rationality is thus radically antinomic. It seems to be attached to the individual, his decisions and actions. In this context it is not, cannot be, intersubjective. The romantic pathos of this does indeed have its roots in the oft-stated awareness which makes the individual—it is for him alone, in his solitude—decide and act according to his "feeling." "Culture," Weber says, "is an area closed off by the meaningless infinity of th future of the world, to which direction and meaning is ascribed from man's point of view. It is such also for men who conflict with a concrete culture as though with a mortal enemy, and who aspire to a 'return to nature.' They can arrive at this position only in that they refer concrete culture to their ideas on value."[8] Yet Weber does not shrink from formulations that at times seem to point to a general characteristic of modern humanity in rationality, one that certainly has its historical roots in Western Europe, but according to a universalistic view that makes one remember a scientistic element, at times clearly technocratic, in the Veblen of *The Place of Science in Modern Civilization*.[9] There are lesser writers, pointless to mention here, representative of a "middle culture"—for instance C. P. Snow, the famous author of *The Two Cultures and the Scientific Revolution*.[10] In *Wissenschaft als Beruf*, Weber says that "from the practical point of view, intellectualistic rationalization directed towards science and scientifically oriented technique does not indicate a general progressive knowledge of the conditions of life surrounding us. Rather, it points to something quite different: the awareness or the belief that everything in principle can be mastered by *reason*. This in turn means the disenchantment of the world. One no longer needs to resort to magic to master or to ingratiate oneself with the spirits, as does the savage, for whom like powers exist. *Reason* and technical means provide this. Above all, this is the meaning of intellectualization as such."[11]

5. The Individual's Social Action

It might be considered that Weber sees the weight of reason in human history as decisive. In reality, this is not so. At least partially and also in the West, social action escapes from its control. For Weber, social action is an individual act that is socialized, by anticipating and reacting to the acts of other people. As he said, "As with any action, social action may also be determined (1) in a rational way as regards the end—by expectations regarding the attitude of objects of the outside world and other men, making use of these expectations as 'conditions' or 'means' for rationally willed and calculated ends, as follows; (2) in a manner rational as regards the value—from the conscious belief in the unconditional value in itself (whether ethical, aesthetic, religious, or interpretable in other ways) of a particular piece of behaviour as such, leaving out from its result; (3) affectively—by sentiments and current states of sensation; (4) traditionally—by an acquired habit."[2]

Talcott Parsons's criticisms on this point manifest a deep misunderstanding (as we have already noted above and elsewhere). Weber is not concerned to construct the total, necessarily reified "social system." He is aware that this would mean freezing history and producing an abstract exercise in modeling: this would possibly help to reorder the data concerning the existing situation, but it would not be possible to take social change into account. The "grand visions," the all-inclusive social systems for Weber, can only be the product of basically useless intellectual exercises. Anyone, he said, with a certain irony, who wants a vision should go to the cinema: on the other hand, anyone who longs for sermons should go to a monastery. These aforementioned comments, which may seem ironic, distant, and tough, are really self-deprecatory, almost reaching the level of pathos. They contain the core, the intrinsic nature of the concept of "disenchantment." In fact, he said, if "the destiny of an age which has eaten of the tree of knowledge is to know that we cannot grasp the meaning of cosmic development on the basis of the conclusion of the investigation however perfectly established,"[13] the consequence is logically inevitable. The responsibility for "meaning," once it has departed from the great traditions, or the authority of the "eternal yesterday" as its basic and essential foundation, rests finally on the individual's decisions. The "meaning" is no longer given: to Weber, we as individuals must be "capable of creating it ourselves."[14]

Because of this fundamental reason and logical bond, Weber speaks of a "polytheism of values," the "right to the unilateral analysis of reality,"[15] and the basic necessity of "presuppositions" declared and decided upon by the individual who undertakes the specific research, so as to succeed in determining what is important and what is not. Rationality is thus handed over to the individual and his presuppositions; as already noted, it appears as a highly antinomic conception, whose meaningful connections are to be found within the general polarity which for Weber is contained in the tension-distinction between material and formal rationality. In most of the areas mentioned above, this tension-distinction involves in particular the economic, juridical sector. Weber said that an economic action "should be *formally* defined as 'rational' to the extent that the 'economic thrust' essential to any rational economy can be interpreted, and should be interpreted, in numerical expressions, of 'calculation,' wholly cutting out the technical formulation of these calculations, and thereby the monetary or natural nature of their estimations. Nonetheless, this conception is univocal, at least in the sense that the monetary form represents the highest level of such *formal* estimability—naturally, all other things being equal. In contrast, the concept of *material* rationality takes on very different meanings. It simply expresses this common element—that analysis is not satisfied with the *fact*, which can be stated in a relatively unequivocal manner, and that there must be a rational calculation as regards the aim, using the most suitable technical means. However, it gives weight instead to the ethical, political, utilitarian, hedonistic requirements *(forderungen)*, those of the stratum of equality, or indeed of any other kind. It measures against them, on the basis of *rationality in regard to value,* or a material goal *(Wertrational oder material zweckrational),* the consequences of economic action (even if this be formally rational and calculable.) One must, however, observe that it is always possible, *in a totally autonomous form* as regards this material critique of the economic effect—a critique which is ethical, aesthetic, and ascetic of the *intention* and *methods* of economic activity *(Wirtschaftsgesimmung sowohl wie cer Wirtschaftsmittel).* The merely formal *(bloss formale)* function of monetary calculation may appear subordinate or outright contradictory *(subaltern oder geradezu . . . feindlich)* with their postulates, when confronted with all these forms of criticism."[16]

Weber also remarks on natural calculation, and the natural economy which historically corresponds to this; that is, an economy which neither knows about nor practises the use of money. As usual, however, he expresses his own thoughts in analytically counterposed conceptual frameworks, returning to rational calculation as capital's calculation, a full and historically unparalleled expression of formal rationality. He does this in order to identify the connections and conditions which actually make it possible. Basically, there are three conditions: "(1) Market competition

(Marketkampf) between economies which are—at least relatively—autonomous. Prices expressed monetarily are the products of struggle and compromise, and thereby the result of clusters of power *(Machtkonstellationen)*."[17] (2) "The highest level of economic activity, as a means of orienting calculation, is achieved by monetary estimate in the form of capital's calculations: this involves the material presupposition of the widest market freedom, in the sense of the absence of monopolies, whether these be imposed from without and economically irrational or voluntary and economically rational (that is to say, directed on the basis of market possibilities)."[18] (3) "Not all 'demand' *(Begehr)* in itself, but demand for useful services based on *buying power, materially* determines—through determination of the calculation by capital—the production of goods in the context of an acquisitive economy. Thus, for the direction of production, the 'constellation' of marginal utility of the social stratum living on unearned income is decisive. This stratum has the power and inclination to acquire a specific service for purposes of utility."[19]

In Weber's outline of these three conditions, the extraordinary awareness of the historic nature of concepts and kinds of economic relation is striking: these, in the tradition of classical economics, seemed natural concepts and processes, and by definition nonmodifiable and metahistorical. If only in passing, the attention Weber pays to money (which is not "an innocuous designation of services of undetermined usefulness, and cannot moreover be arbitrarily altered without fundamentally affecting the nature of the prices established by the struggle between individuals") introduces a completely political and sociological element into the discussion of this theme; the theme is largely regarded as ideally "indifferent" and purely technical and is not yet confronted by modern monetarists. Witness of this is the work of Milton Friedman and the discussions inspired by him.

Weber's analysis is not limited just to the discussion of macroeconomic conditions. It follows an examination of the motives which in a market economy are the "decisive stimulus for economic actions." To understand fully the structure of these motivational pressures, as well as to avoid any lapse into the purely psychologistic level, Weber clearly conceptualizes—almost running the risk of schematic presentation—the distinction—tension between market economy and planned economy. In brief, one can say that in his view, although in a market economy "the activity of particular, autonomous forms of the economy is directed also autonomously . . . in a planned economy, on the other hand, every economic activity is directed, *insofar as it is realized, in conformity with the domestic economy,* heteronomously, on the basis of regulations which command and prohibit, as well as on the basis of a perspective of rewards and punishments."[20] In the context of the market economy, the stimulus to economic activity is represented by three motivations: "(1) For the have-nots, by the coercive force of the risk of a total lack of supplies for themselves and their dependents (children, wives, and ultimately parents), for whom the individual must typically provide, as well as, in various degrees, by an internal predisposition to economic work as a form of life; (2) For those who actually enjoy a position of privilege, because they have possessions or education (in turn determined by possessions), the stimulus comes from possibilities of high incomes, ambition, and the value conferred on prized types of 'profession' (spiritual, artistic, technical, etc.); (3) For those who take part in the possibilities of acquisitive enterprises, the stimulus comes from the risk of their own capital and their own opportunities for gain, in connection with the 'professional' disposition towards rational acquisition. That is the case insofar as this is seen as a "proof"*(Bewahrung)* of the service itself, and as a form of autonomous domination over the people who depend on instructions from them, and also control over possibilities of supplying the wants of an indeterminate mass of individuals; their instructions thereby have importance for their culture or their lives— in short, as a form of power."[21]

6. Formal Rationality, Material Rationality, and Planning

Let us suppose that instead of a market economy there is, and operates, a planned economy. What would its results for structure and psychological-motivational "disposition" be? First, Weber notes that there would be a certain lessening of coercion derived from the risk of a lack of supplies. A planned economy would not, in fact, be able to discharge onto its dependents the results of a potentially lesser service from the worker. Equally, the autonomy of enterprises' management would diminish, with a subsequent lessening, probably to zero, of the risk to capital, with the apparently inevitable recourse to "idealistic stimuli of an altruistic nature." Yet at the same time, a planned economy would also have to face up to a more or less radical diminution of formal rationality, basically linked with monetary calculation and that of capital. There thus arises the problem of the practical realization of socialism, in the sense that *formal* rationality based on an estimate regarding capital which allows rational accountability, and *material* rationality, which obeys ethical needs and those of postutilitarian justice, differ from each other so greatly that there arises an irreconcilable contradiction which, in turn, reflects the basis of the "irrationality of the economy which is one of the roots of any social problematic, above all that of socialism."[22]

It is, however, more in the political sphere than in the economic and juridical ones, that those characteristics which split up the seemingly unitary nature of modern society become explosive and reach breaking point. They arise as an impassable obstacle. The process of rationalization broadens out here into the formation of formal bureaucratic orders, from which there grow contradictions, oppositions, which in Weber's analysis seem irreconcilable. Of the three pure types of legitimate power, the bureaucratic type would at first sight seem the one logically tied to rationality. In fact, Weber convincingly outlines its characteristics and presuppositions—rational and impersonal—as a "cosmos of abstract rules and norms established accordingly," regarding the value, ends, or both, as against the other two types of power, traditional and charismatic. One might say that with the advent of legal, bureaucratic power in the formal sense, with a rational character insofar as it "rests on the belief in the legality of decreed regulations, and on the right to command of those called upon to exercise [legal] power on the basis of these," the process of rationalization finally triumphs. Meanwhile, complementarily, on the strictly political plane, on the ruins of the ancient social orders dominated by aristocratic, dynastic orders, mass democracy and the modern "social" state are proclaimed; that is, alternatively, the entrepreneurial, planning, all-administering state. Bureaucratic structure is more than ever necessary. Legal bureaucratic power is inconceivable without its administrative apparatus. Furthermore, with its characteristic depersonalization of functions and, simultaneously, the specialization of responsibilities, bureaucratic structure seems basically to cling to the egalitarianism of democracy and its intrinsic need for impersonal rotation and socialization of power. The egalitarianism of the bureaucracy, however, is formal: that which underlies democracy is substantial, unless one wishes to reduce the concept of democracy to a simple ensemble of formal procedures, independent of socioeconomic content, on the basis of the principle that he who desires democracy must be content with this (this is the conclusion drawn by most American politologues [Lipset, Dahl, Polsby, etc.], and also by the Europeans, who follow the same course with minimal variations [Lepsins, Crozier, Bobbio, Sartori, etc.]).

In fact, as Weber never tired of pointing out, bureaucracy tends to involve society in its entirety, and to deprive politicians of their function, by routinizing them and depriving them of authority. The instrument for removing this authority, which foreshadows the atrophy of political judgment, is specialized knowledge. This is at the root of the institution of specific power (one only controls what one knows), and of the social figure of the bureaucrat. In fact, the specific mode of functioning of modern bureaucracy, in his view, rests on certain general "principles": "(1) the principle of the spheres of *competence* of definite authorities, disciplined in a general manner through rules: that is, through administrative laws and regulations; (2) the principle of the *hierarchy of offices,* and the series of procedures—a rigidly regulated system of supra- and sub-ordination of the organisms of authority with control of the superiors over their inferiors; (3) modern office management is based on documents (agreements) which are preserved in the original or in duplicate, and on an apparatus of subaltern and clerical functionaries of all kinds; (4) every official activity normally presupposes meticulous specialized preparation; (5) official activity claims the whole of the bureaucrat's working capacity; (6) the office procedure of the functionary follows general rules which can be learned. The knowledge of these rules is thus a special technique which functionaries have."[23]

7. The Sociopolitical Consequences of Specialized Knowledge

Modern techniques and the economics of the mass production of goods leave specialized knowledge out of consideration. Man thus cannot escape domination by the bureaucracy, since it is precisely that, in a form indissolubly linked to material, or at any rate objective, interests, which ends up by determining individual conditions of existence. The legal functionary type therefore seems left out of the great socio-historical upheavals;

as far as Weber is concerned "power", and "leaders" change, but the "function" of bureaucracy, its "specific technique" of performing all the duties of power, remains. It is transformed but cannot be eliminated. The potency that such a specialized knowledge in the bureaucracy involves, in reality increased by the competence acquired on the job (from which there is derived the concept of the "official secret," analogous to the commercial secrets of the firm), only the capitalist entrepreneur can oppose.[24]

The private interest in profit can, indeed, in the context of its own interest, alone attain the specialized knowledge and awareness of things that can free him from the dominance of the rational wisdom of bureaucracy, which thereby becomes a tool in his own hands. Elsewhere, the bureaucracy, out of the need to be able to choose freely the best-qualified functionaries, creates within itself the conditions for bringing about a certain kind of leveling: it tends, too, to create the "power of formalistic impersonality" which allows it to discharge in a purely technical manner—as regards "anyone"—the objective duties involved in a particular department. As we have seen, there are two basic characteristics to Weber's bureaucracy: "permanence," and the function of "rationalization." Once in being, bureaucracy becomes the hardest form of social structure to overthrow. Elsewhere, it represents the most suitable means for transforming "community action" into "social action," rationally ordered. It is at the same time an imposing instrument for "socialization" in the hands of whoever has control of the bureaucratic apparatus.[25] Any mass resistance is bound to succumb in the face of the characteristic indispensability of a "continuous," "functioning," "impersonal" apparatus. The bureaucratic phenomenon, apart from having its own social and economic conditions, is also able to generate them; this is especially the case where the distribution of power and the direction provided to the apparatus of those who use its powers are involved.[26] The rationalizing function of this structure permits an understanding of the current and potential capacity of political and industrial capitalism, as against Marx, for whom the system of the capitalist economy is dominated by internal contradictions and class conflict.[27]

8. Charisma and Routine

The confines of the formalism and routinization of bureaucratic procedures did not, however, escape Weber's notice. The concept of "charismatic power" also helps Weber to counterbalance certain consequences of the exercise of bureaucratic power. Especially in relation to events in Germany during and after the First World War, Weber concludes by posing the dilemma of bureaucracy—presented as lying between the alternatives of organizational efficiency and the formalization of conflicts, characteristic of every sociological experiment, and observation of the phenomenon: the problem, in short, of the relations between bureaucracy and bureaucratization, or "between the development of organizations which promote and facilitate the achievement of certain ends. They provide services, fully performing important functions, but are in contrast with the phenomenon of an ever-increasing absorption of uncontrollable powers from the side of those organizations."[28] Weber sees bureaucracy as a compendium of rationality and technical efficiency — an autonomous body, full of beneficent power destined to rationalize the life and activity of society; but it is in actuality the concept of "rationalization" that is problematic for him, and thus does not seem sufficiently clarified.

Using Mannheim's famous distinction,[29] we can say that Weber left obscure the differentiation between a functional type of rationalization as technical efficiency, and "substantial" rationalization. He was certainly aware of, and could demonstrate, the differences between some forms of ancient bureaucracies and the modern organization of industry and public administration, but it is also the case that to use the measure of efficiency and productivity so plainly more than once could be of little assistance in evaluating and promoting rationalization. One may argue that Weber ends by counterposing to the undervaluation of the bureaucratic phenomenon on the part of historical materialism, a symmetrical position; it is, however, one of the opposite kind, employing a kind of rationalistic overestimation of the phenomenon. In modern society the growing process of bureaucratization takes place simultaneously with the process of socialization. This process—for Weber—is irreversible, and he sees it as highly improbable that there can be any working-out of means suitable for containing it. Nonetheless, for Weber, this is what should be attempted, in order to conserve part of "free humanity" and bring individuals to an awareness of their rights. This could provide hope for a new, different "meaning" to give to the unstoppable "bureaucratic travail," and lessen the dangers of hypostases in terms simply of calculation, efficiency, and productivity. Possibly only in some remarks by Nietzsche, with whose work Weber was familiar, are there critical demands as passionate as they are tormented concerning the "bureaucratic travail," like those which the theorist of bureaucratic power was setting forth after the *Protestant Ethic,* Weber said that "the Puritan *wanted* to be a professional, whilst we *have* to be. Just as ecstasy was taken from monastic cells to professional life and began to dominate lay existence, it helped to build the powerful economic order—linked to technical and economic presuppositions about mechanical production—which now determines extraordinarily strictly the style of life of each individual. Perhaps it will continue to do this until the last ton of coal is burnt: to determine the life-style of everyone born in this system, not only those taking part in purely economic activity. Concern for material possessions should—for the 'chosen'—be wrapped around like a light cloak, easily thrown off, in Baxter's view. However, destiny made that cloak a steel cage."[30] This concern recurs pressingly and still more dramatically as a persistent leitmotif in Weber's political writings. Weber, in regard to the form of method, rejects any "substantial" *(substanzielle)* notion of collective groupings, in order to start from, and preserve in his analysis, the individual *(Einzelindividuum).* Here, too, in regard to the aimless perfection which in his view seems an essential characteristic of bureaucratic-formal orders, typical of technically advanced societies on the way to being totally administered (to use Horkheimer's formulation), Weber's analysis easily overcomes the limits of a simply psychosocial phenomenology in order to frequently broaden out into "structural explanations"; that is, to expand into proposition at the basis of which it is a social formation, not an individual, which determines certain consequences for itself and other social formations. In the 1909 assembly of the *Verein für Sozialpolitik,* Weber noted that if "we look at a purely technical, efficient administration as the peak and sole ideal, one may certainly say—to hell with anything else. Think of the effect of this total bureaucratization and nationalization which we now see approaching. Every worker is measured in this calculation like a cog in the machine, and increasingly from within he is thus compelled to feel like this, to ask himself only if perhaps from being a small wheel he might one day become a big wheel. It is as though in politics the craze for order—in the perspective wherein those Germans who thought they were acting for the best will end up—was enough to decide everything. It is as though only through knowledge and will *must* we become men who serve 'order' and nothing but order, and who become nervous and scared as soon as this order wavers for a second, and become helpless as soon as they are uprooted from this total incorporation into order. Let us hope the world does not know that these 'sons of order' are the evolutionary development to which we are constantly despatched."[31]

Weber perceives, therefore, and plumbs the depths of a purely instrumental rationality, but he does not have the technical nor the methodological means to solve it. He would rather stoically analyze it, with great coldness and the academic modesty characteristic of him. His project of offering us a global vision of everything involved—as simultaneously cause and effect—in the makeup of the social is unquestionably fascinating. His limitations, however, are equally undeniable. They are plain in the very title of his major work: not *"Economy"* Against, Under, Before, or After *"Society,"* but *Economy* and *Society*. That is, we have the economic framework together with the cluster of varied, multidimensional, contradictory social facts in equilibrium, at the same level, with a tendency to stand fast, if not frozen; despite their antinomies they remain in unstable equilibrium. Only the will, the projects of chance individuals ("charismatically") possessed by the "Catilinarian rage" of the demon for action, will be able to set these things in motion unpredictably, or by means of an inscrutible "destiny."

It may seem paradoxical that the theorist of the modern world as a *totally calculable* world should arrive at such a conclusion. This is also, however, the proof of rigorous intellectual honesty which led him to reject the illusory promises of "sacrificed" history, and the formulations of ideological speculations passed off as intersubjectively binding scientific certainties. It is the attitude of the sociologist who rejects consolatory shortcuts and who is satisfied with the role of the impartial and unbending witness to the crisis. Among the many duties of sociology, what Weber never accepted, still less advocated, was consolation at all costs.

9. Max Weber's Limitations

The richness and depth of Weber's analyses are beyond question. There is, however, still a question regarding what has been mentioned in the third part of this work: from the podium of his university chair and as a political journalist, Weber, a committed intellectual, did not foresee the rise of Nazism. With the introduction of Article 48 into the Weimar Constitution, one might even argue that unconsciously he assisted it.

How could such an eventuality occur? How could this famous scholar, who was so troubled by scruples concerning the accuracy of documents involving ancient Eastern religions to the point of losing sleep over them, so grossly fail when there was a question of the political future of his country? What is the hidden reason for this complete blindness which seems to cloud quite unexpectedly Weber's extraordinary analytical acuteness?

The surprising element is still more evident if we think about the disturbing fact that, in regard to the details of the European political and cultural situation, Weber gave ample proof of exceptional perspicacity. He foresaw the fragmentation and political segmentation that would result from adopting the law on proportional representation. He had no illusions, and indeed described extremely accurately the emergence of and the sociopsychological type of the professional politician, who no longer lived for politics but off it. He is more analytical than Marx but also more so than Werner Sombart in regard to industrial complexes and bureaucratic hyperdevelopment. He never tired of presenting typologies of the city, endless catalogues of activities and social types, definitions, distinctions and subdistinctions of strata, conditions, and power. All this is destroyed by the simple sociopolitical, economic, and cultural reality of post-Wilhelmine Germany. While the great sociologist was settling out his typologies with cultured intelligence, a former house painter and frustrated artist would soon be writing *Mein Kampf* and expressing in it the fear and anguish of a defeat that was never accepted and recognized as such—the desire of a whole people which felt it had been cheated of victory, and thirsted for new conquests.

To understand both the merits and limits of the method and substance of Weberian sociology, this question is basic. It is, however, a question that is never clearly raised. Even the most incisive commentators tend to draw from Weber's deep well all the materials which, by chance, they happen to need, without thinking of the construction of the whole—with the same merry thoughtlessness with which the medieval church builders ravaged the temples of classical antiquity. Teachers are usually destroyed by their disciples, and Weber did not escape this rule. We have already referred to Talcott Parsons's approach, which basically sees in Weber no more than his own forerunner. For Parsons, Weber began the construction of the general theory of the "social system" and intentionally directed action. Too bad, Parsons seems to say, that Weber stopped halfway. There is no surprise, therefore, in that it is up to Parsons to take up the cudgels and complete the task. Naturally, this is a total misunderstanding. Parsons is facing problems that do not even marginally enter into the problematic context of Weber's interests. Weber is faced with the problem of change or at least the reorientation of an elite —an economic summit—social and political, summoned by the increasing power of a Germany reunited by Bismarck to measure up to its real historic stature: its own suitability in regard to the needs of rational direction and optimal use of human and material resources—clearly on the increase—so as to break definitively the traditional balance of power in Europe, established at the Congress of Vienna and already flawed by the 1870 Franco-Prussian War. Parsons has to discharge, more or less consciously, a quite different function.

Even before 1940—the *Structure of Social Action* dates from 1936[32] —but especially during the years immediately following the Second World War, Parsons, setting himself up as the interpreter of the reemergence of a systematic claim from the social sciences, quietly began a discussion that perfectly suited the deepest needs of American society. There is no doubt that in both his tenor of thought and his life-style, Parsons belonged to the descendants of the great cultural systematizers and the "lay popes." However, one needs to see these things at close range. The America which was a victor in the Second World War was radically different from the America of the prewar period. "O Pioneers" of Walt Whitman's verse was far in the past; the crude simplicity of the pioneers, their domestic virtues, —a memory tinged with rhetoric—the innocence of a whole New World, beyond the complicated contanglements of conflicting ideologies and the defiling struggles of power politics, was lost for ever.

Almost by surprise, America found itself after the Second World War in an essentially new position, now distant from any concrete possibility of isolationism, immediately involved in world affairs. It was an uncomfortable position, to which middle Americans and the ruling class itself were unaccustomed, but it was inevitable. Once Wilson's moralism and rigid Puritanism had spent itself in the immediate postwar period, the United States had been able to return to their normal framework, having obviously made good bargains. Having entered the war in 1917 when the die was already cast, with few casualties and, all in all, little bother, they managed to go from being a debtor nation (especially in respect to France and England) to being the creditor nation among their nearly moribund, starving allies. Once the armistice was signed, American soldiers, strategists, and statesmen had been able to abandon Europe and return peacefully to their own domestic concerns, leaving behind at most a little elite of writers in Paris and thereabouts who were to have a ball at least until the great crash of 1929, when the collapse of industrial shares on Wall Street and the adverse exchange rate of the dollar were, somewhat brusquely, to close the splendid Parisian interlude of Gertrude Stein, F. Scott Fitzgerald, Ernest Hemingway and the other talented expatriates. In this context, despite its meannesses—especially in regard to Fitzgerald—we should remember Hemingway's *A Moveable Feast*, required reading on this phenomenon.

The period after the Second World War was radically different. The United States emerged in a hegemonic position on the world scene and could no longer simply go home. In this profoundly altered situation, one can grasp the deep purpose and the reason—not by chance—for Talcott Parsons's destiny. His work became emblematic. The construction of the "social system" and the identification of its functional prerequisites might appear to be a purely theoretical undertaking in intellectual terms. In reality, it was the reply to a complex political need that postwar American felt in its most sensitive nerve endings, in the tormenting sense of a new, unspoken imperial responsibility that Britain's decline placed on American shoulders and made the nation feel insecure. Still it provided an emotional sensation, though one already perceived as an inevitable result, or a kind of murky penalty, of the war that the nation would be unable to go home and barricade itself within, forgetting the Old World and its complicated intrigues and irresolvable problems. The United States was forced to face up to the external world—the "un-American" world. It was no longer a question of choice but a question of survival. Beyond ideological confrontation and considerations of empire, there were only irrelevance and historical destruction. The nation had to acknowledge itself, settle on its own identity in order to present itself as a credible point of reference, and an ideal assembly or meeting point for the ideological loyalty of human beings.

Parsons's "social system" represents the visiting card of the U.S.A.; that is, it is the toughest, most mature attempt that the country made to recognize and identify itself—the attempt, so to speak, to "reflect itself" in a systematic construct at a high level of abstraction, in which the basic principles of the common life, analytically justified and guaranteed against any possible development, are laid down and established forever. This is done as a reply, an exorcism of the danger of falling apart before making contact with the "outside world," with "other" cultures.

The complex political need for self-analysis and self-affirmation that the postwar United States beats is double: it has an internal and external dimension. On the internal level, the need shows itself in the necessity for homogenization, integration, so that the nation does indeed become an effective "union," not simply as a juridical entity (our more perfect Union—as a society of immigrants, of blacks and whites, people of radically different racial and religious origins, and of profoundly conflicting interests, beneath the official credo of equality). On the level of international and intercultural relations, the postwar United States has not only to resolve the problem of the photogenic projection of its own image. For this, the tale of the returning immigrants, those who in some way made their fortune in "God's own country," would perhaps suffice. Rather, there is a question of presenting America as a determinate historical reality, while simultaneously making it tend toward, or coincide with, the absolute, atemporal model of an industrally advanced, technically progressive society. This would be done so that it might join on to and identify itself with, ultimately, the only civil society believable these days, empriically identifiable and at the same time normative in ideal terms for all possible societies. The confusion, typically American, between datum and value, becomes clear in this perspective: the confusion that is, between what is and what *ought to be*. In addition, the inability —typically American—to see one's self as others see us, to accept the otherness of the other, also becomes clear; that is, one sees the imperialistic "missionary" tendency to want to reduce the other to one's own image, to project oneself, one's values and culture, on to what is other than oneself. They are projected on to other cultures, other different values, so denying—along with the pluralism of cultures and values, the dialectic and history. So, they eternalize themselves, with the level of development historically determined and attained, as though it were the ultimate, absolute level, the terminus of history, the end of the evolutionary potential of humanity and of the economic, political, and cultural stage of our common life. At the same time, it refuses in the specific historical and political reality to understand others and to have relations with peoples and cultures which are other than those of direct or indirect domination.

Behind Parsons's systematic exposition, there thus emerges the double political need of the United States to integrate and cohere within, and at the same time to assert itself hegemonically at the level of international relations. The task Weber assigns himself is quite different. The rationalism he sees as the distinctive mark of the West; and which he views as truimphing in the major bureaucratic organs and the rise of the modern state, should not be confused with the "instrumental activism" of which Parsons speaks. For Weber the concern and basic preoccupation lie in the raising of a responsible political elite, independent of the major bureaucrats who lack responsibility in the full sense of the word; for Parsons political tension has already collapsed and been diminished to the extent that political direction and administrative practice can be passed off as one and the same thing.

10. Weber and the Dialectic

It thus should be clear that it is impossible to see Weber as the premise for Parsons's systematic framework. The inadmissability of this conception rests on two basic orders of reasoning. The first concerns the specific historical context to which the two writers belong and their responses to the different requirements they seek. We have already mentioned these reasonings. The second, on the other hand, lies in the intrinsic logical motives on which, however schematically, we ought to dwell. In this light, we should first point out that Weber, in clear contradiction with Parsons's purpose, nowhere shows any interest in building a "system." The sense of historical specificity is very much alive in him. Weber prefers to concentrate on the real changes in Western history rather than to set about constructing a general theory of development or social change or "social system." In other words, he prefers an empirical science of concrete realities to an abstract system of global, undefined societies; the specificities of given, lived, historical life to a vague, timeless universalism. It is, however, true that Weber speaks of "causal law" *(Kausal Gesetz)*. In my view, however, Weber's 'causal law' has nothing to do with the tendential general laws of the historical school, nor with the equally general or even generic evolutionary principles of Spencer—nor finally, with the evocative parallels, the "orders and re-orders," or the spurious generalizations of the "philosophers of history," who constantly confuse principles of personal preference with scientific testing.

The problematic here indicated is important, and can certainly not adequately be dealt with in the brief space allotted here. Weber's "causal law" is one of imputation, a genetico-causal attribution, which thus tends to delineate and disentangle the causal-conditional interconnections between phenomena. It is, however, a causal law which is strictly relative and limited to a specific, well-defined, and circumscribed historic context. It is thus not valid "in general," or in other, different contexts, save by analogy, but only within a particular environment—that is, within a precise "historical horizon" (e.g., the phenomenon of capitalism within Western—only Western—history). From this there descends Weber's basic idea, which has been so widely misunderstood, of the historical *individuum* or *unicum* as the *grounding object* of *comprehending* sociology. Weber's historical *individuum* is not the unique, irreducible, unrepeatable, and thus unpredictable, *ineffable* historic event of idealist historicism (from Dilthey and Rickert to the Italian neoidealists, especially Croce and Antoni). If it were thus, the very notion of sociology as science of the historic human event, would immediately collapse. This "event" is stated in terms of its elements of relative uniformity and so, inasmuch as it is never either absolutely determinate or indeterminate, but variously conditioned, predictable, it still exists within the somewhat narrow margins of the specific conditions which indeed weigh upon every meaningful human activity, activity directed toward an end. Thus, for Weber, the event—intentional human action—is not ineffable or unforeseeable, but, rather, may be chosen and presented as the object of scientific analysis.

Having said this, it must at once be made clear that Weber's causal law does not fall into the classical ambiguities of the positivistic notion of the social fact—thanks precisely to the intentionality of human action with which it is concerned and which by definition escapes the "factualistic" petrification of the naively positivistic kind. Once, however, that we have demonstrated, or at least referred to, the difference between Weber's causal law and the historicist-idealist and positivist conceptions, we cannot state that Weber launches a historico-dialectical analysis. Louis Schneider has recently noted that "a dialectical view does not necessarily contain a dubious metaphysics of culture or history, and should not assume that the universe itself exudes a solution for the major social problems of man, a solution which will involve certain happiness. It may be compatible with an empirical tendency which demands proofs of dialectical propositions and may very well not be satisfied with a proposition simply because it has a dialectical form or argument. It is this type of dialectic, which is certainly not in conflict with science, which seems to me clearly to figure in Weber's thought."[33]

It seems fair at this point to express some doubt. If one could prove the well-groundedness of Schneider's interpretation, the advantages would be obvious. A dialectic in agreement with science would offer above all a way out of the old Popper-Adorno impasse. The doubt, however, arises that from the term and concept of dialectics there follows here a strongly, improperly, reductive meaning. Weber was always attempting to construct analytical typologies, catalogues, and inventories accurate enough to run the risk of the accusation of pedantry. At any rate, it seems clear that for Weber every law, type, or catalogue relating to historically specific, sociologically meaningful phenomena cannot be divorced from its intrinsically *formal* nature. In contrast, for instance, with Marx or Hegel, Weber seems to be convinced that objective reality cannot be "latched on to," as it were, by means of conceptual schemes (whence the charge—not without foundation—of neo-Kantianism).

One might also point out, even though this appears somewhat difficult, and certainly wearisome, that Weber, in his actual research procedure and style of layout, would not seem to be a dialectical sociologist; that is, that he did not act and proceed from the basis of an assumption concerning a really dialectical motion in global social reality. His typologies (patrimonialism, bureaucracy, etc.) align elements of reality, abstract typifications, real—historically determinate, selected and subsumed— phenomena within a conceptual scheme intended to guarantee their methodical, rational reordering. This would thus provide conceptual understanding, instead of purely subjective perception, as it were, Dilthey's version of *Erlebnis*. Yet these elements, aspects, or facets which correspond to the theoretically infinite modes whereby reality presents itself to us like a prism, and which Weber has the great merit of not reducing, petrifying, and constraining into the old mechanistic "factors," he never sees as dialectically interacting in the strict sense. He collects them all on the same level—possibly for reasons of maximum scruple for heuristic impartiality—and refuses to assert the priority of any one over another. He stops himself from recognizing any privileged elements, and thus condemns himself to a paralysis, to shortsightedness, even blindness, in regard to the dynamic of the present to which he was so attached and to whose study he devoted all his energy. Indeed, to go further, through this taste for accurate analytical typology, tending toward completeness, and all-inclusive, Weber is basically retrospective. His analyses help us to understand the past. They are more or less silent about the present. In the last analysis, Weber, too, is paralyzed by an "excess of history," to use Nietzsche's phrase. We may discern in him foreshadowings of a new dialectic, able to link empirical data and conceptual universality, and to grasp through the conception of sociology as a participation of researchers and objects of research, history in its making. For Weber, however, to set out such a new "relational dialectics' completely, he would have had to transcend, along with his family and social origins, his deeply rooted elitism. This elitism was entrenched at the theoretical level, and in existential experience, in his methodological individualism, his tragic political vision, wholly permeated with an unconquerable mistrust of the masses at the very moment he saw with dazzling clarity the historic inadequacy, the technical shortfall and the mental backwardness of the elite in power.[34]

NOTES

1. M. Weber, *Wissenschaft als Beruf*, It. trans.; *Il lavoro intellettuale come professione*, Turin: Rinaudi, 1977, pp. 17-18.
2. M. Weber, *Wirschaft und Gesellschaft*, It. tr *(Economy and Society); Economia e Società* Milan: Ed. di Comunita, 1961; 2 vols.
3. L. Strauss, Diritto naturale a storia (Natural Right and History), passim, esp. p. 57 ff. Venezia: Neri Pozza, 1957.
4. Cf. M. Weber e il desting della regione, Bari, Laterza, 1973, p. 91.
5. T. Parsons, *Il sistema sociale*. Milan, Ed. di Comunità, 1965.
6. M. Weber, *Die Verhaltnisse der Landarbeiter in ostelbischen Deutschland (The Social System)*, Tubingen, Mohr, 1958.
7. Cf. D. Cantimori, Introductory remarks to M. Weber, *Il lavoro intellettuale come professione*, op. cit., p. 15.
8. Cf. F. Ferrarotti, *Trattato di sociologia (An Alternative Sociology), p. 255.* Turin, Utet, 1968. See also F. Ferrarotti, introduction to A. Comte, *Corso di filosofia positive*. Turin, Utet, 1967 (this was earlier published as"*La sintesi sociologica nel pensiero di Comte,"* in *Cuaderni di sociologia*, April–June, 1966); cf. also my *Società come problema e come progetto*. Milan, Mondadori, 1979.
9. M. Offenbacher, *Confession und soziale Schichtung*. Tubingen, 1901.
10. Cf. E. Sestan, Introduction to M. Weber, *L'etica protestante e lo spirito del capitalismo (The Protestant Ethic and the Spirit of Capitalism)*, Florence, Sansoni, 1977, p. 36.
11. Sestan, op. cit., p. 27.
12. P. Ammassari, *Il rapporto fra biografia e storia in Hans Gerth e C. Wright Mills, La critica sociologica*, p. 11. Automn 1969, p. 51 (my emphasis).
13. Weber, *L'etica . . . (The Protestant Ethic), op. cit.,* p. 79 (quotation marks in original).
14. M. Weber, *Il metodo delle scienze storico-sociali (Max Weber on the Methodology of the Social Sciences)*, pp. 61-62, Turin Einaudi, 1967. *(Spaces in original.)*
15. Among the many commentators and critics, perhaps the only one to grasp this aspect of Weber's work was Max Rheinstein, formerly his student in Munich. Rheinstein, *Max Weber on Law in Economy and Society,* p. xxxii. Cambridge, Mass., 1954. "*Economy and Society* is a powerful attempt to give us a typology and complete classification of important social phenomena, and to explore their interconnections."

CHAPTER TWO

1. This evidence and Weber's statements are recalled in the painstaking, useful book by Nicola M. De Feo, *Introduzione a Max Weber,* Bari, Laterza, 1970, pp. 51-52.
2. M. Weber, *Die Protestant sche Ethik,* . . ., It. trans., *L'etica economica delle religioni mondiali,* Appendix 11, to F. Ferrarotti, op. cit., pp. 243-244, now too in Weber, *Sociologia della religioni (The Sociology of Religion).* Turin, Utet, 1976.
3. The concept of "social action" or of "acting in society" is really the key concept in Weberian sociology. One notes that Weber uses the verb, not the noun *(Handeln,* not *Handlung)* to refer to the fluid nature of behavior that the term denotes. Social action is the action of an individual who, however, in deciding his modes of action and his desired end, takes into account the reaction in the past, present, and future, or in any case foresees and in some way assumes the behavior of other individuals. Acting in society is our reaction toward other people, not simply acting together with other people or under their influence. For example, only those actions or behavior are not social that lie within the personal control of the actor, e.g., religious ecstasy, unless one exploits such a state to influence people. Thus it is not social action to win a victory in a tennis match unless by winning the game the winner gains a prize for himself, fame, and prestige for his country. For a summary definition, see Weber, *Il metodo delle scienze storicosociali,* pp. 262-274. For a clear example, see ibid., pp. 271-272, "A convenient example to illustrate the succession from occasional association to union regarding a goal is offered by the development of industrial cartels, from the simple agreement reached once on the limits of the minimum selling process by individual competitors, to the syndicate, supplied with its own wide powers, with sales offices and a complex apparatus of organisms. Common to them all is merely the stipulated ordering whose content, conforming to the explicit determination presumed here in an ideal-type form, contains at least the indication of what must be ordered, or conversely excluded, or even allowed by the participants." For the four types of social action, see Weber, *Economia e società,* vol. 1, p. 23.
4. M. Weber, *L'etica economica delle religioni mondiali,* p. 244 (my emphasis).
5. See M. Weber, *L'etica protestante e lo spirito del capitalismo (The Protestant Ethic. . .),* p. 77.
6. Ibid., p. 245 (emphasis in original).
7. W. Sombart, *Il capitalismo moderno.* Turin, Utet, 1967.
8. Weber, *L'etico protestante* . . . , pp. 67-68.
9. Weber, *Economia e società, (Economy and Society),* p. 165 (spacing in original).
10. Weber, *L'etica protestante.* . . , pp. 100-104.
11. Ibid., p. 88.
12. On this whole question, see F. Ferrarotti, *Trattato di sociologia,* especially the third part, "Verso l'autonomia operativa del guidizio sociologico," chap. 3, *Razionalismo, capitalismo e potere,* pp. 155-192.

13. Cf. Weber, *L'etica protestante...*, pp. 96-97.
14. Ibid., p. 137 (emphasis in original).
15. For a fuller treatment of the concept of *Beruf*, see Ferrarotti, *Trattato*, p. 159 ff.
16. M. Weber, *L'etica protestante...*, pp. 177-178.
17. Ibid., p. 179.
18. Ibid., p. 192.
19. See also in this regard Chapter 4 of the present work.
20. See H. Lüthy, *Le passé présent: combats d'idées de Calvin à Rousseau*. Monaco: Editions du Rocher, 1965 (It. edn., *Da Calvino a Rousseau*, Pologna: Il Mulino, 1971). Kurt Samuelsson's *Economia e religione*, Rome, Armando, 1973, should not, however, be overlooked.
21. B. Cantimori, op. cit., p. 12.
22. Luthy cites *en passant* the name of Nef, but does not repeat the titles of his basic works on the coal industry in England at the time of the first industiral revolution, nor yet *Cultural Foundation of Industrial Civilisation* (Cambridge: CUP, 1958), which would provide valuable material for the support of his interpretation.

CHAPTER THREE

1. See in this regard, F. Ferrarotti's observations in *Trattato di sociologia*, especially the paragraph *Potere, forza, cominio*, p. 175 ff.
2. See in this regard, F. Ferrarotti and others, *Stuci e ricerche sul potere*. Rome, Ianua, 1980.
3. Weber permits himself an observation of an unusual spitefulness in a note on 'charismatic power' where he says there is also a charisma which needs 'speculators.'
4. M. Weber, *Economia e società*, vol. 1., p. 211 (spaces in original).
5. Ibid., p. 240 (emphasis in original).
6. Ibid., pp. 241-242.
7. See W. J. Mommsen, *Max Weber und die deutsche Politik, 1890-1920*, Tübingen, Mohr, 1959.
8. See Weber, *Gesammelte politische Schriften*, p. 382. Tübingen, Mohr, 1958.
9. On this theoretical and existential limitation of Weber, see F. Ferrarotti, introduction to *Sociologia del potere: de prerogativa personale a funzione razionale collettiva*, Bari, Laterza, 1976. It is a disturbing symptom in the current crisis of "Western Marxism" that the "political" is theorized as being "autonomous" and that the thought of Carl Schmitt should be more or less surreptitiously taken up by Marxists like Tronti and others.
10. See V. Loewenstein, *Max Weber's Political Ideas in the Perspective of Our Time*, Amherst, University of Massachusetts Press, 1966, p. 17.

128 / NOTES

CHAPTER FOUR

1. M. Weber, *Sociologia delle religioni (The Sociology of Religion)*. Turin, Utet, 1976.
2. Ibid., p. 130 (quotation marks in original).
3. Ibid., p. 89 (emphasis corresponds to spacing in original).
4. Ibid., p. 42.
5. Ibid., p. 101.
6. Ibid., p. 101 (emphasis corresponds to spacing in original).
7. Ibid., p. 102.
8. Ibid., p. 328 (emphasis corresponds to spacing in original).
9. Ibid., p. 891 (quotation marks in original: emphasis corresponds to spacing in original).
10. Ibid., pp. 891-892 (quotation marks in original: emphasis corresponds to spacing in original).
11. Ibid., p. 604.
12. Ibid., pp. 761-762 (quotation marks in original: emphasis corresponds to spacing in original).
13. Ibid., pp. 121-122.
14. See F. Ferrarotti, *Max Weber e il destino della ragione*.
15. M. Weber, *Sociologia delle religioni (The Sociology of Religion)*. p. 102. (My emphasis).
16. Ibid., p. 585 (my emphasis).
17. Ibid., p. 585-586 (quotation marks in original; my emphasis).
18. Ibid., p. 593-594 (quotation marks in original; my emphasis).
19. Ibid., pp. 595-597 (quotation marks in original; my emphasis).
20. Ibid., p. 400 (quotation marks in original).
21. Ibid., pp. 497-498 (my emphasis).
22. T. Veblen, *Imperial Germany and the Industrial Revolution* (it. trans. in Opere, Turin, Utet, 1969).
23. Karl Marx, *Capital*, Vol. 1, chap. 8, "The Working Day."
24. M. Weber, *Sociologia delle religioni (The Sociology of Religion)*, p. 499, note.
25. See F. Samuelsson, *Economia e religione*.
26. I basically agree in this regard with the remarks by Benjamin Nelson and S. N. Eisenstadt, for which see C. Y. Glock, and P. E. Hammond, eds., *Beyond the Classics: Essays in the Scientific Study of Religion*. New York: 1973.
27. M. Weber, *Sociologia delle religioni*, p. 122 (quotation marks in original).
28. Ibid., p. 155.
29. Ibid., pp. 163-164.
30. Ibid., pp. 165-166.
31. Ibid., p. 178.
32. For Tawney's position, which only partly coincides with Weber's, see my *Introduction to R. H. Tawney. Opere*. Turin, Utet, 1975.

33. See H. M. Robertson, *Aspects of the Rise of Economic Individualism: A Criticism of Max Weber and His School*, Cambridge, Cambridge University Press, 1933.
34. See A. Fanfani, *Cattolicesimo e protestantesimo nella formagione del capitalismo moderno*. Milan: Vita e Fensiero, 1944.
35. See W. Cunningham, *Saggio sulla civilta' occidentale nei suoi aspetti economici*, Florence, Vallecchi, 1954.
36. J. Savary, *Le parfait négociant ou Instruction générale ce cui regarde le commerce de toute sorte de marchanoise, tant ce France cue des pays étrangers*. 1675.
37. H. Lúthy, *Le passé présent: combats d'idées de Calvin a Rousseau*.
38. W. Sombart, *Il capitalismo moderno*.
39. With special regard to the notions of "individualism" and "modernity," see E. Troeltsch, *Il protestantesimo nella formazione del mondo moderno*, Florence, La nuova Italia, 1968.
40. In terms of the negative effects for psychotherapy of the dualistic conception of Calvinism which divides men into the elect and the damned, see M. Rotenberg, "The Protestant Ethic Against the Spirit of Psychiatry: The Other Side of Weber's Thesis," in the *British Journal of Sociology*, Vol. VI, No. 1, March 1975.
41. C. Antoni, *Dallo storicismo alla sociologia*. Florence: Sansoni, 1973.
42. See in this respect the remarks of R. K. Merton, *Science, Technology and Society in Seventeenth-Century England*, especially chapter 4. New York: 1970.

CHAPTER FIVE

1. See J. Huizings, *The Twilight of the Middle Ages, (L'autunno del Medioevo)*, p. 264. Florence: Sansoni. 1978.
2. See M. Weber, *Economia e società, (Economy and Society)*, Vol. 1, p. 505. Milan, ed. Communità, 1968.
3. For the cultural bases of the process of industrialisation, I should like to mention the work of the historian of the English coal industry at the time of the first "industrial revolution," J. U. Nef, *The Cultural Foundation of Industrial Society*. Cambridge: Cambridge University Press, 1958; for a further treatment of this problem, see F. Ferrarotti, *Macchina e uomo nella societa' industriale*, Turin, ERI, 1962.
4. See R. Bendix, "Max Weber's Sociology Today," in *International Social Science Journal*, vol. xvii, no. 1, 1965.
5. M. Weber, *Sociologia delle religioni, (The Sociology of Religion)*, Turin, UTET, 1976, pp. 1161 and 1234.
6. See chapter 4.
7. See S. N. Eisenstadt, *The Protestant Ethic Thesis in Analytical and Comparative Context*, New York: Random House, 1966. Note, too, the introduction by L. Cavalli to M. Weber, *Religione e società*, Bologna, Il Mulino, 1968. For an accurate

130 / NOTES

interpretation, often methodologically oriented, see J. A. Pradès, *La sociologie de la religion chez Max Weber.* Louvain, Nauwelaerts, 1969.
8. See Weber, *Il Metodo delle scienze storico-sociali,* Turin, Einaudi, 1967.
p. 96. Also *The Methodology of the Social Sciences,* New York, Free Press, 1949.
9. T. Veblen, *The Place of Science in Modern Civilization.* New York, Huebsch, 1919.
10. C. P. Snow, *Le due culture e la rivoluzione scientifica,* (The Two Cultures and the Scientific Revolution), *Milan, Feltrinelli, 1970.*
11. See M. Weber, *Il lavoro intellettuale come professione,* Turin, Einaudi, 1977. p. 19 and p. 20. (Emphasis in original).
12. M. Weber, *Economia e societa',* pp. 21-22.
13. M. Weber, *Il method delle scienze storico-sociali,* cit., p. 64
14. Ibid.
15. Ibid., p. 83.
16. Weber, *Economia e societa',* vol. 1, pp. 80-81 (emphasis corresponds to spacing in original).
17, Ibid., p. 103.
18. Ibid., p. 104.
19. Ibid.
20. Ibid., p. 105 (emphasis corresponds to spacing in original).
21. Ibid., p. 106 (emphasis corresponds to spacing in original).
22. Ibid., p. 107.
23. M. Weber, *Economia e societa',* Vol. 2, pp. 260-262.
24. At the beginning, the coming of the charismatic leader may reduce or overthrow the existing type of bureaucracy. Later, it turns out that the latter acquires new force according to the strength of the requirement to observe the duties the "new law" imposes.
25. One should remember in this context the famous criticism of the "indefinite progress of the bureaucratising tendency," lately convincingly set out by R. K. Merton. We must, however, look elsewhere for the valid aspect of Weber's insight in having pointed out a common, indeed isomorphic, tendency in capitalism and socialism as rational systems.
26. An important fact regarding modern capitalist bureaucracy is its relative independence from state bureaucracy. The latter has characteristics in common with military organization, as the modern army has a pronounced bureaucratic character, in contrast with feudal armies, for example. It is important, however, that two of the most characteristically capitalist societies (including those of older origins), England and the United States, are in fact those in which the army has a minor influence on social structure as compared with the major European states. These facts show that capitalist bureaucracy has an independent development. (See. T. Parsons, *La strutture dell'azione sociale,* Bologna, Il Mulino, 1962, p. 626.

27. The principle of the separation of the laborer from the material means of exercise of authority is wholly accepted by Weber, and use of this principle allows for a broader and deeper analytical extension applicable to a wider number of phenomena. It is "common to the modern state's exercise of power and to its civilization in the political and military sense and to private, capitalist industry. In both cases, the disposability of these means is in the hands of the power to which the design of the bureaucracy conforms. This design is characteristic of all these organizations, and its existence and function is indissolubly linked, both as cause and effect, with the concentration of the material means of its exercise." Again, "the hierarchical dependence of the worker, the shop assistant, the technician, the government or military functionary, rests on a totally technical foundation. For the instruments, supplies, and the financial means indispensable for the maintenance and independence of the economy are concentrated for deployment on the one hand by the entrepreneur, and on the other, by the political leader or government." See M. Weber, *Parlamento o governo nel nuovo ordinamento della Germania*, p. 23, Bari, Laterza, 1919.

28. S. E. Eisenstadt, *Bureaucracy and bureaucratisation in Germany*, in *Current Sociology*, vii, 2, 1958, p. 103.

29. K. Mannheim, *L'uomo e la societa in una eta' di ricostruzione*, Milan, Ed. Comunita', 1959, pp. 50-79.

30. M. Weber, *Sociologia delle religioni*, vol. 1, p. 321.

31. M. Weber, *Scripti politici*, pp. 112-115. Gatania, Giannotta, 1970.

32. T. Parsons, op. cit.

33. L. Schneider, *Max Weber: Saggezza e scienza in sociologia*, in *Rassegna italiana di sociologia*, xi, 4, October-December, 1970, pp. 536-537.

34. As a first step toward the construction of a 'relational dialectic' I refer the reader to my *Storia e storie di vita*. Bari, Laterza, 1981.

SELECTED BIBLIOGRAPHY

I. WORKS BY MAX WEBER IN ENGLISH TRANSLATION

Note: Professor Ferrarotti often cites the original German or Italian edition in his text. The date of the German edition is supplied in parenthesis for integral books.

Ancient Judaism (1917). Glencoe, Ill.: Free Press, 1952.
The City (1894-1896). Glencoe, Ill.: Free Press, 1958.
Economy and Society (1922). Edited by Guenther Roth and Claus Wittich. Berkeley: University of California Press, 1979.
From Max Weber: Essays in Sociology. Translated by H. H. Gerth and C. Wright Mills. New York: Oxford University Press, 1946.
General Economic History (1890). Translated by F. H. Knight. Glencoe, Ill.: Free Press, 1950.
Max Weber on Law in Economy and Society. Edited by Max Rheinstein. Cambridge: Harvard University Press, 1954.
Max Weber on the Methodology of the Social Sciences (1922). Translated by Edward Shils and H. A. Finch. Glencoe, Ill.: Free Press, 1949.
The Protestant Ethic and the Spirit of Capitalism (1904). Translated by Talcott Parsons. London: Allen and Unwin, 1930.
The Rational and Social Foundations of Music (1921). Carbondale: Southern Illinois University Press, 1958.
The Religion of China: Confucianism and Taoism (1915). Glencoe, Ill.: Free Press, 1951.
The Religion of India: The Sociology of Hinduism and Buddhism (1916). Translated by H. H. Gerth and Don Martindale. Glencoe, Ill.: Free Press, 1958.
Roscher and Knies: The Logical Problems of Historical Economics (1903-1906). Translated by Guy Oakes. New York: Free Press, 1975.
Selections in Translation. Edited by W. G. Runciman. Translated by E. Matthews. Cambridge: Cambridge University Press, 1978.
The Sociology of Religion (1921: posthumous). Translated by Ephraim Fischoffs. Boston: Beacon Press, 1964.
The Theory of Social and Economic Organization (1917). Translated by A. M. Henderson and Talcott Parsons. Glencoe, Ill.: Free Press, 1957.

BIBLIOGRAPHY / 133

II. WORKS BY WEBER CITED IN OTHER LANGUAGES

Gesammelte politische Schriften (1921). Tübingen: Mohr, 1958.
Il lavoro intellettuale come professione (1919). Turin: Einaudi, 1977.
Scritti politici. Catania: Gianotta, 1970.
Die Verhältnisse der Landarbeiter im ostelbischen Deutschland (1892). Tübingen: Mohr, 1958.

III. PRINCIPAL SECONDARY SOURCES

Note: A title with an asterisk indicates that it is a reprint of an earlier translation and edition.

BOOKS

Comte, Auguste. *Introduction to Positive Philosophy*. Indianapolis: Bobbs-Merrill, 1970.
Cunningham, William. *An Essay on Western Civilization in Economic Aspect*. 2 vols. New York: Scribner's, 1898-1900.
De Feo, Nicola M. *Introduzione a Max Weber*. Bari: Laterza, 1970.
Eisenstadt, S. N. *The Protestant Ethic Thesis in Analytical and Comparative Context*. New York: Random House, 1966.
Fanfani, Amintore. *Catholicism, Protestantism and Capitalism*. New York: Arno, 1972.
Ferrarotti, Franco. *Introduction to R. H. Tawney*. Turin: Utet, 1975.
–––. *Studi e ricerche sul potere*. Rome: Ianua, 1980.
–––. *Max Weber and the Destiny of Reason*. Armonk, N.Y.: M. E. Sharpe, 1982.
–––. *Trattato di sociologia*. Turin: Utet, 1968.
–––. *Societa come problema e come progetto*. Milan: Mondadori, 1979.
–––. *Sociologia del potere: da prerogativa personale a funzione razionale collettiva*. Bari: Laterza, 1976.
Glock, Charles Y., and P. E. Hammond, eds. *Beyond the Classics: Essays in the Scientific Study of Religion*. New York, 1973.
Huizinga, Johan. *The Twilight of the Middle Ages*. New York: Doubleday, 1978.
Loewenstein, Karl. *Max Weber's Political Ideas in the Perspective of Our Time*. Amherst: University of Massachusetts Press, 1966.
Lüthy, Herbert. *Le passé présent: combats d'idées de Calvin à Rousseau*. Monaco: Editions du Rocher, 1965.
Mannheim, Karl. *Man and Society in the Age of Reconstruction*. New York: Harcourt, Brace, 1940.

134 / BIBLIOGRAPHY

Marx, Karl. *Capital.* New York: Modern Library, 1936.
Mommsen, Wolfgang J. *Max Weber und die deutsche Politik, 1890-1920.* Tübingen: Mohr, 1959.
Nef, J. U. *The Cultural Foundation of Industrial Society.* Cambridge: Cambridge University Press, 1958.
Offenbacher, M. *Konfession und soziale Schichtung.* Tübingen: Mohr, 1901.
Parsons, Talcott. *The Social System.* Glencoe, Ill.: Free Press, 1964.
Robertson, Hector M. *Aspects of the Rise of Economic Individualism: A Criticism of Max Weber and His School.* Cambridge: Cambridge University Press, 1933.
Savary, J. *Le parfait négociant ou Instruction générale ce que regarde le commerce de toute sorte de marchandise, tant de France que des pays étrangers.* 1675.
Snow, C. P. *The Two Cultures.* Cambridge: Cambridge University Press, 1969.
Sombart, Werner. *Modern Capitalism.* Benjamin Franklin Press, 1969.
Strauss, Leo. *Natural Right and History.* Chicago: University of Chicago Press, 1965.
Troeltsch, Ernst. *Il protestantesimo nella formazione del mondo moderno.* Florence: La Nuova Italia, 1968.
Veblen, Thorstein. *Imperial Germany and the Industrial Revolution.* Ann Arbor: University of Michigan Press, 1966.
Veblen, Thorstein. *The Place of Science in Modern Civilization.* New York: Russell, 1961.

JOURNALS

Ammassari, P. "Il rapporto fra biografia e storia in Hans Gerth." *La critica sociologica.* No. 11, Autumn 1969.
Bendix, R. "Max Weber's Sociology Today." *International Social Science Journal.* Vol. XVII, No. 1, 1965.
Eisenstadt, S. N. "Bureaucracy and Bureaucratisation in Germany." *Current Sociology.* Vol. VII, No. 2, 1958.
Rotenberg, M. "The Protestant Ethic against the Spirit of Psychiatry: The Other Side of Weber's Thesis." *British Journal of Sociology.* Vol. IV, No. 1, March 1975.
Schneider, L. "Max Weber: Saggezza e scienza in sociologia." *Rassegn italiana di sociologia.* Vol. XI, No. 4, 1970.

INDEX

Adorno, Theodor W., 8, 20, 123
Alberti, Leon Battista, 95-96
Antoni, Carlo, 34, 96, 122

Bales, Robert, 100
Baxter, Richard, 35, 97, 115
Bellah, Robert, 51
Bendix, Reinhard, 14, 102-103
Bergson, Henri, 75
Bismarck, Otto von, 61, 118
Bobbio, Norberto, 112
Brecht, Bertolt, 38
Brentano, Lujo, 69, 94
Bunyan, John, 49
Burke, Edmund, 72
Burresi, Pietro, 74

Calvin, John, 35, 47-49, 52, 91, 97, 102
Cantimori, Delio, 18-20, 51
Carlyle, Thomas, 67
Cavalli, L., 129 n. 7
Columbus, Christopher, 52
Comte, Auguste, 11, 14, 17-20, 22
Copernicus, Nicolaus, 52
Croce, Benedetto, 75, 122

Crozier, Michel, 112
Cunningham, W., 95

D'Annunzio, Gabriele, 63
Dahl, Robert, 112
Darwin, Charles, 62, 75
DeFeo, Nicola M., 126 n. 1
Dilthey, Wilhelm, 22, 122, 124
Durkheim, Emile, 8, 11, 15, 17, 44, 101

Eisenstadt, Samuel N., 36, 50, 103
Emerson, Ralph Waldo, 67
Engels, Frederick, 19, 30-31, 41, 77, 81
Erasmus, Desiderius, 52
Fanfani, Amintore, 94

Fitzgerald, F. Scott, 119
Franklin, Benjamin, 34, 42-43, 52, 80, 95-96, 105
Friedman, Milton, 109
Fugger, Jakob, 52, 96, 105

Geertz, Clifford, 51
Gentile, Giovanni, 75
George, Stefan, 61

136 INDEX

Gohre, Paul, 69
Gramsci, Antonio, 54
Guttman, Julius, 50

Halbwachs, Maurice, 11
Hegel, G. W. F., 91, 123
Hemingway, Ernest, 119
Hitler, Adolf, 73, 117
Homan, George C., 100
Huizinga, Johan, 99
Husserl, Edmund, 75

Jonadev Ben Rekav, 81

Kant, Immanuel, 19, 101, 123
Katz, J., 50

Labriola, Antonio, 75, 77
Landshut, Siegfried, 51
Lepsins, 112
Liguori, Alfonso de, 50
Lipset, Seymour M., 112
Lukacs, George, 77
Luther, Martin, 47-48, 52-53
Luthy, Herbert, 51-54, 95

MacLelland, 61
Mann, Thomas, 61-62
Mannheim, Karl, 114
Marcuse, Herbert, 20, 92
Marinetti, Filippo Tommaso, 63
Marx, Karl, 11, 19, 27, 30-31, 33, 41, 57, 75-77, 82, 86, 88-92, 101, 103, 117, 123
Mauss, Marcel, 11
Medici (family), 52
Merton, Robert K., 130 n. 25
Michels, Roberto, 30
Mohammed, 81
Mommsen, Theodor, 13
Mommsen, W. J., 69

Naumann, Friedrich, 69
Nef, John U., 52, 127 n. 22, 129 n. 3
Nelson, Benjamin, 128 n. 22
Nietzsche, Friedrich, 68, 101, 115, 124

Offenbacker, Martin, 21, 54

Papini, Giovanni, 75
Pareto, Vilfredo, 30, 80, 92
Parsons, Talcott, 3-4, 10, 100, 107, 118-121
Paul, Saint, 68
Peguy, Charles, 75
Polsby, Nelson W., 112
Popper, Karl, 123
Prades, J. A., 129-130 n. 7

Rheinstein, Max, 125 n 15
Rickert, Heinrich, 21, 22, 122
Riesman, David, 24
Robertson, H. M., 94
Rotenberg, M. Fordecchai, 129 n. 40

Saint-Simon, Comte de, 11, 19
Samuelsson, Kurt, 92-93, 95
Sartori, Giovanni, 112
Savary, Jacques, 52, 195-96
Scheler, Max, 75
Schmitt, Carl, 127 n. 9
Schmoller, Gustav, 69
Schneider, Louis, 123
Schopenhauer, Arthur, 93
Schulze-Gavernitz, 69
Sestan, Ernesto, 20-21, 23, 51, 74
Shils, Edward A., 100
Singer, Milton, 50-51
Smelser, Neil, 100
Snow, C. P., 106
Sombart, Werner, 37-38, 93, 95-96, 105, 117
Sorokin, Pitirim A., 80
Spencer, Herbert, 15, 75, 101, 122
Stein, Gertrude, 119
Steiner, George, 63
Stocker, Adolph, 69
Strauss, Leo, -, 8

Tawney, R. H., 38, 94
Taylor, Frederick Winslow, 49
Tocqueville, Alexis de, 72
Toennico, Ferdinand, 20, 29

Treitschke, Heinrich von, 8, 69
Troeltsch, Ernst, 129 n. 39

Van der Sprenkel, O., 50
Veblen, Thorstein, 24, 25, 86, 91, 106

Wagner, Adolph, 69

Walkley, Mary Anne, 92
Weber, Marianne, 13, 24
Wilson, woodrow, 24, 119
Windelband, Wilhelm, 21, 22
Wittfogel, Karl, 90

Yang, C. K., 50